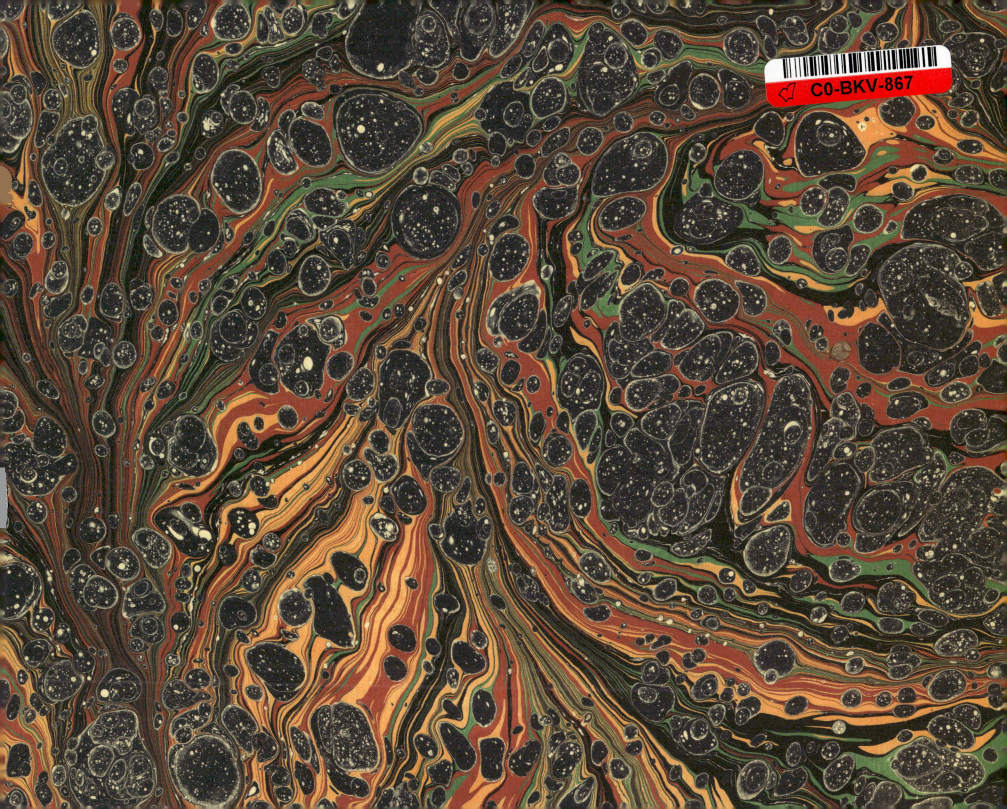

Eagles and Anchors

The Belts and Belt Plates

of the

U.S. Navy and Marine Corps

1780-1941

Peter Tuite

Schiffer Military History
Atglen, PA

Printed in China.
ISBN: 978-0-7643-4342-1

We are interested in hearing from authors with book ideas on related topics.

Published by Schiffer Publishing Ltd.
4880 Lower Valley Road
Atglen, PA 19310
Phone: (610) 593-1777
FAX: (610) 593-2002
E-mail: Info@schifferbooks.com.
Visit our web site at: www.schifferbooks.com
Please write for a free catalog.
This book may be purchased
from the publisher.
Try your bookstore first.

In Europe, Schiffer books are distributed by:
Bushwood Books
6 Marksbury Avenue
Kew Gardens
Surrey TW9 4JF, England
Phone: 44 (0) 20 8392-8585
FAX: 44 (0) 20 8392-9876
E-mail: Info@bushwoodbooks.co.uk.
Visit our website at:
www.bushwoodbooks.co.uk
Try your bookstore first.

Contents

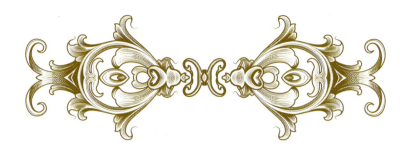

ACKNOWLEDGMENTS

When I started this book three years ago, I was a collector of U.S. Navy belts and plates, and it wasn't clear to me that the subject warranted a book – particularly in color. The journey has been a real learning experience. I met many collectors I hadn't known before, read books on belts and plates by prominent authors, and looked at museum and collector pieces that were truly unique and never before seen. There are many people to thank, but the person who encouraged me and kept me plodding along was my friend Jack Bethune, who reviewed and commented on almost every word, and basically kept me on the straight and narrow. There were also a number of other collectors who took the time to review and comment on individual chapters or sections. These included Bruce Bazelon, Lt. Colonel Charles Cureton, John Gunderson, George Juno, and Earl Scheck. All provided valuable inputs and contributed to the quality of the final product.

There couldn't be a book without the help and input from collectors and institutions. Some institutions provided access to their entire collections and enabled the author to include pieces that have never before been published. Jim Cheevers of the U.S. Naval Academy at Annapolis (USNA) led the list of institutional contributors, providing access to all the Preble Museum's archived belts and plates. Kathy Grant of the Smithsonian Institution provided photographs of the unique USMC material at the American History Museum (AHM), and Neil Abelsam and Joan Thomas provided photos from the National Museum of the Marine Corps collection. Kathy Wright, of the Museum of the Confederacy (MOC) and the Virginia Historical Society (VHS), provided photographs of the unique CSN items in their collections. The Nantucket Historical Association also provided photos.

The project could not have been completed without access to original copies of U.S. Navy and U.S. Marine Corps uniform regulations. This access was provided by Jennifer Bryan at the U.S. Naval Academy library, Tanya Simpson at the Washington Navy Yard library, and Suzanne Christoff at the U.S. Military Academy library. The New York Historical Society library provided copies of the original versions of the USMC 1839 and 1859 regulations.

Some collectors also made their naval pieces available to the author for photography, while others forwarded photographs of items in their collections. These contributors included Bruce Bazelon, Jack Bethune, Sim Comfort, Norm Flayderman, Jack Frost, John Gunderson, Kevin Hoffman, and Dr. Allen D. Phillips. Jerry Roxbury found the unique CSN belt and plate owned by Brooks Holder, and Michael Florio provided two wonderful naval portraits. Special thanks go to Dexter Fabian, a graphic designer in St. Petersburg, Florida, who did the layouts and got the manuscript ready for publishing.

Thanks to my oldest grandson, Michael, who found the War of 1812 Congressional belts in the Naval Academy archives. Special thanks to my wife Claudette, who read all the text (she's the English major) to make sure the final product was reasonably intelligible.

Peter Tuite

6

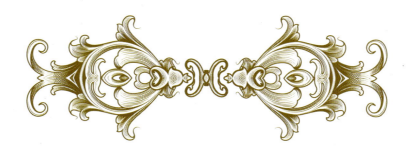

LIST OF PLATES AND IMAGES

Chapter

I

INTRODUCTION

The belts and plates worn by U.S. naval officers evolved to the state of uniformity finally achieved in 1941 over a period of about 150 years. The early shoulder belt plates and waist belt plates were true works of art, each one being different, and their designs were consistent with the independent nature of the officers who wore them. As the Navy attempted to standardize what officers wore, the designs employed for a given pattern, although varied, were similar. From 1790 through about 1830, just about any belt plate that had an eagle or anchor on it was worn. Even after the Navy issued its first pattern belt plate in 1830, with the eagle and anchor, officers were still flexible in the belts and plates they wore. When the second pattern went into effect in 1841, there was less flexibility. The release of the third pattern belt plate in 1852 essentially eliminated flexibility. With the Civil War and its large influx of naval officers, it was almost impossible to find an image of a period naval officer not wearing a pattern belt plate. The 1852 pattern plate design, with eagle and nearly horizontal anchor, essentially remained in effect through 1941, when the Navy changed the direction the eagle was facing. After the Civil War, most of the changes prescribed for officers' belts and plates involved dress belts, which were used to distinguish rank.

This book attempts to take the reader on a journey of belts and plates from about 1790 through 1941. The emphasis is on the color photography, which depicts both the belt plates and, in many cases, the belts that were worn. There are over one hundred and fifty color illustrations, many of them composites of two, three, or four different photographs that show every aspect of a particular belt plate. Many of the items illustrated have never been published and could only be seen in private collections, or in the storage rooms of museums. The Navy regulations that relate to the requirements for belts and plates are also presented in abbreviated form throughout the text, complete with their own graphics in Appendix A.

The first five chapters are devoted to the U.S. Navy. Chapter 6 covers the hat plates and belts and plates worn by the U.S. Marine Corps from about 1800 through 1859. The Navy and Marine Corps regulations governing USMC belts and belt plates are used throughout the text and are presented in their entirety in Appendix B.

Another subject that has not yet been completely addressed is that of the belts and plates worn by Confederate naval officers. This subject is addressed in Chapter 7, and includes all known belt plate designs.

Chapter

2

EARLY BELTS AND BELT PLATES

One of the first acts of the Continental Congress was the establishment of a navy, and the Continental Navy was born on 13 October 1775. Although there were uniform regulations for Continental naval officers, their accoutrements were relatively simple, and to a large extent followed those worn by French and British naval officers, belt and shoulder plates included. The Continental Navy did, however, prescribe buttons, and the button prescribed for Lieutenants in the Continental Navy [1] was an anchor (2.1).

The Continental Navy was disbanded immediately after the war, and its last ship was sold in 1785. It wasn't until 27 March 1794 that Congress finally passed the legislation that led to a U.S. Navy being formed.[2] The Navy's first set of Uniform Regulations was issued in 1797.[3] These regulations prescribed uniforms and buttons, but no mention is made of belts and plates. The prescription for buttons was simply: *Buttons, yellow metal, and to have the foul anchor and eagle on the same.* None of the buttons prescribed in the 1797 regulations are extant. As we will see in subsequent chapters, the Navy did not prescribe belts or belt plates in its regulations until 1830. Accordingly, naval officers were free to wear the belts and plates of their choice that were being provided by merchants of the time. This practice continued through 1830 and for some time thereafter. Continental naval officers seemed to have favored the use of shoulder straps, both with and without plates, to carry their swords. Some of the earliest naval plates known are examples of these shoulder plates. They were primarily imported from England, and many of those surviving are marked with the Francis Thurkle cartouche, a stamped FT. Thurkle was a prominent London supplier of naval swords, dirks, and naval shoulder plates.[4] He founded his firm in 1766 and he died in 1801.

2.1 Continental Navy anchor button. (Bruce S. Bazelon)

Portrait of Captain Charles Pole with anchor shoulder plate. (Michael Florio, Quester Gallery)

2.2 Thurkle anchor shoulder plate. (N. Flayderman)

2.3 Captain Broke Thurkle's anchor shoulder plate. (Sim Comfort)

The first observed naval shoulder plate (2.2) is a relatively large once-gilded oval with a fouled anchor. This was a common naval motif used by American and British naval officers. This plate retains some of its gilt and the anchor is elaborately engraved. The plate rear has two studs and a hook soldered to it for attachment to the belt. It also has the stamped *FT* cartouche. A very similar plate by Thurkle was worn on a shoulder strap by Captain James Broke, a prominent British naval officer who commanded the *HMS Shannon* during the War of 1812. This plate, on its shoulder strap, is shown (2.3). The fouled anchor is identical to the plate above, but the edges of this plate are engraved with a cross hatched motif.

There are two similar British shoulder plates with anchors on exhibit at the National Maritime Museum in Greenwich, England, and are shown on their website. One of these was made specifically for a British unit, has the Thurkle cartouche, and is dated 1794. The other one is a simple fouled anchor like that shown above and marked with a *B*, but its maker remains unknown. The eighteenth century portrait of Captain Charles M. Polk (Royal Navy) shows him wearing a shoulder belt plate with anchor like those shown above. In 1782, Polk commanded the frigate *HMS Success* as Captain and was made Admiral of the Blue in 1799.

2.4 Unmarked anchor shoulder plate. (John A. Gunderson)

2.5 Silver shoulder plate with eagle, anchor, and cursive USN. (Dr. Allen D. Phillips)

2.6 Armitage shoulder plate. (Dr. Allen D. Phillips)

A similar shoulder plate not made by Thurkle with a fouled anchor is illustrated (2.4). This plate has a different style finely engraved fouled anchor motif that is surrounded by a rope border. It is similar in size to the other ones, but except for the rope surround, there is no evidence of gilt. Like the ones above, the rear has the identical two stud and hook arrangement for belt attachment, but does not have any maker marks. This plate would also pre-date 1800.

These early naval shoulder plates were more elaborate than just anchors. An engraved oval silver shoulder plate from the same period with USN on it is shown (2.5). This plate has a large primitive American eagle with shield sitting on an unfouled anchor with USN below in script. A simulated rope border surrounds

the periphery. The rear has the identical two stud and hook arrangement for belt attachment like the others, but there are no maker marks.

The Navy issued another set of uniform regulations in 1802,[5] but belt plates were not mentioned. However, the prescription for buttons was modified to read: *the buttons of yellow metal, with the foul anchor and American eagle, surrounded with 15 stars.* A shoulder plate with a design that is similar to the button regulation is illustrated (2.6). This gilded oval plate made by Thurkle is engraved with an eagle on a branch looking over his right shoulder holding a shield with fouled anchor on his left wing and surrounded by 16 six pointed stars. As shown, the design motif is separate and attached with five mounts through the oval plate. Like the other shoulder plates, the back has two studs

with a hook, and like the first one, it has the *FT* cartouche. This design motif was prepared by George Armitage of Philadelphia, among others. Armitage was a Sheffield silver plate worker and maker of military trimmings as early as 1798, and buttons in 1799.[6] He was also a sword hilter, and continued in these businesses until 1826. An example of this design motif on a sword hilt[7] with Armitage's initials, GA, is illustrated (2.7). Several other manufacturers employed the same design. This same motif with 16 six pointed star surround was also used on buttons as early as 1798, and a button with this design that dates to 1802 is also shown (2.7). Thurkle died in 1801, but his son continued in the business and could have used the father's famous cartouche on this Thurkle shoulder plate with eagle and shield. Alternatively,

since the eagle with shield design was in use shortly after the Navy was formed in 1798, the 1802 button regulation could have post dated this plate.

This same design motif was also used on what appears to be a dirk belt plate (2.8). This plate is cast and, while the fouled anchor is no longer present, the eagle with shield on branch with 16 six pointed stars remains intact. This plate would date to the early 1800s.

Examples of what types of plates were in use during the War of 1812 can be seen in early portraits of prominent naval officers. The portrait of William Bainbridge[8] shows a relatively wide elaborate belt with large eagle plate, and the famous portrait of Samuel Chester Reid[9] shows a plain black belt with a large silver eagle plate. The Navy would continue to use the eagle and some form of anchor for its belt plates right through the present day. Conversely, the portrait of Oliver Hazard Perry shown has him wearing a large round silver belt plate.

The next series of naval belt attachment devices are not really plates in the true sense

2.8 Armitage dirk plate. (Bruce S. Bazelon)

– they are clasps with an S shaped hook closure. An early example of an eagle based belt plate is shown (2.9). An example of a dug plate with the same design is also shown. Due to its size, this was probably from a dirk belt, as this eagle motif can also be found on some early naval dirk cross guards. There are several of these plates extant, so this was probably a popular dirk belt design for its time.[10]

There is another series of belt clasps that embody the eagle and anchor motif. The first

2.9 Double eagle head plate with dug head inset. (Dr. Allen D. Phillips)

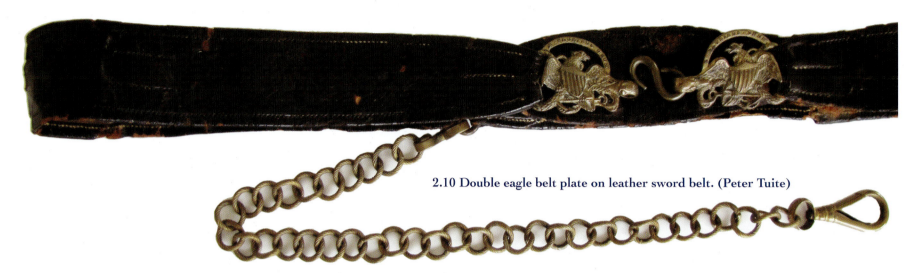

2.10 Double eagle belt plate on leather sword belt. (Peter Tuite)

Portrait of Oliver Hazard Perry wearing a silver belt plate. (Michael Florio, Quester Gallery)

is a leather sword belt (2.10) with simple eagle clasp and S hook closure. The facing eagles on the clasps (2.11) are sitting astride an anchor and snake with a shield on their breast and a semi-circular *e pluribus unum* banner above. The belt is 1 ½ inches wide, tapers at the clasps, and has two chain sword straps with hooks. It is die struck and gilded.

A more elaborate version of the same clasp design is shown on the leather dirk belt illustrated (2.12). This belt is 1/2 inch wide. In addition to the same eagle clasps (2.13), this dirk belt has three slightly smaller eagle connectors, two with chain straps. The device at the connectors is the same,

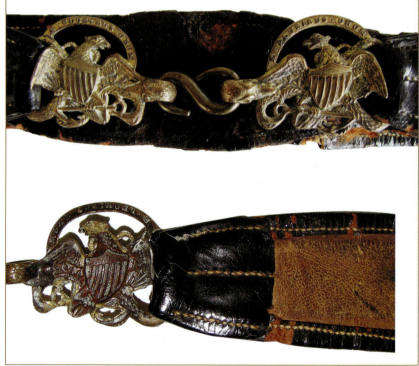

2.11 Double eagle sword belt plate details. (Peter Tuite)

2.12 Double eagle leather dirk belt. (Peter Tuite)

2.13 Double eagle dirk belt plate details. (Peter Tuite)

2.14 Comparison of double eagle plates. (Peter Tuite)

exclusive of the banner above. Another dirk belt with identical clasps without the leather has been previously published,[11] indicating that this was a popular design. A comparison of the clasps from each belt (2.14) shows different dies being used, which is indicative of more than one maker.

The next plate example (2.15) shows a blue silk dirk belt with less elaborate facing eagle clasps and snake S hook. These eagle designs (2.16) are similar to those above, including the motifs on the eagle's right and

2.15 Double eagle belt plate on blue silk dirk belt. (Peter Tuite)

2.16 Compairson of double eagle dirk plate details. (Dirk plate above, Peter Tuite)

Lake Champlain, and the two single ship engagements between USS *Sloop Peacock* and HMS *Epervier* and the USS *Wasp* and HMS *Sloop Reindeer*. About seventy-seven swords were made and distributed between 1816 and 1822.[14] Each sword was accompanied by the red Moroccan leather belt with gold embossing shown (2.18). This belt belonged to Sailing Master Thomas Brownell (USN 1812-1815, 1840-1867),[15] who served on the *USS Ariel* during the battle of Lake Erie. The large plate with Neptune's head (2.19) is a false one, and is riveted to the belt; the actual clasp is to its right as shown.

left wings. Again, the plates are die struck and gilded.

These die struck facing eagle design motifs with S-hook would seem to have been fairly common in the 1810-1820 time frame, as two others with almost identical devices are known.[12] All of these eagle devices are also similar to those shown on early buttons.[13] A much larger version of a belt plate with facing eagles on anchors can be seen on the CDV that shows an unidentified older naval officer in a c1850 naval uniform wearing his somewhat older large eagle belt plate.

Another use of the eagle motif, a single eagle with S hooks on either side, is shown in Plate 2.17. This plate, with reverse snake clasp, is a stylized version of the ones described above. The eagle is facing its heraldic left with shield on its chest and is perched on a branch with a furled seven star banner below. This plate was die struck with a fine die, and it has been postulated that the quality of the work necessarily means it was imported. While the die detail is relatively fine, it is no finer than that shown in Plate 2.14.

During the War of 1812, Congress awarded Congressional swords to the Sailing Masters and Midshipmen who participated in four naval engagements. These included the battles of Lake Erie and

CDV of naval officer wearing a double eagle belt plate. (Martin Oogjen III)

19

The Brownell belt is missing its sword straps, but these are shown in a second example of this belt (2.20) belonging to Midshipman James Bliss (USN 1814-1816).[16] These are believed to be the only two belts surviving with the original red Moroccan leather. A third belt plate on black leather belonging to Midshipman William Boden, who received a sword and belt for the battle of Lake Champlain, is at the Shelburne Museum in Vermont.[17]

The next example shown (2.21) is the tongue portion of a cast plate made in the 1820-1830 time frame and is match marked 28. The design motif is an eagle facing its heraldic right on top of an anchor. This plate is believed to be from a militia unit known as the Sea Fencibles. These units were first formed in England during the war with France as a volunteer militia charged with guarding the coast. Several groups of Sea Fencibles[18] with similar duties were formed in this country during the War of 1812.

2.18 Thomas Brownell Congressional Plate details... (U.S. Naval Academy Museum)

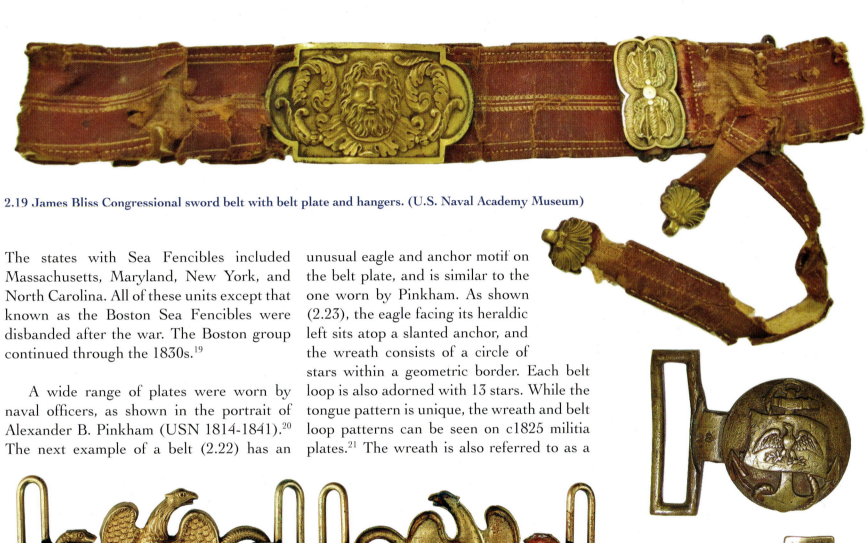

2.19 James Bliss Congressional sword belt with belt plate and hangers. (U.S. Naval Academy Museum)

The states with Sea Fencibles included Massachusetts, Maryland, New York, and North Carolina. All of these units except that known as the Boston Sea Fencibles were disbanded after the war. The Boston group continued through the 1830s.[19]

A wide range of plates were worn by naval officers, as shown in the portrait of Alexander B. Pinkham (USN 1814-1841).[20] The next example of a belt (2.22) has an unusual eagle and anchor motif on the belt plate, and is similar to the one worn by Pinkham. As shown (2.23), the eagle facing its heraldic left sits atop a slanted anchor, and the wreath consists of a circle of stars within a geometric border. Each belt loop is also adorned with 13 stars. While the tongue pattern is unique, the wreath and belt loop patterns can be seen on c1825 militia plates.[21] The wreath is also referred to as a

2.20 Single eagle clasp belt plate. (Dr. Allen D. Phillips)

2.21 Sea Fencible's belt plate tongue. (Peter Tuite)

21

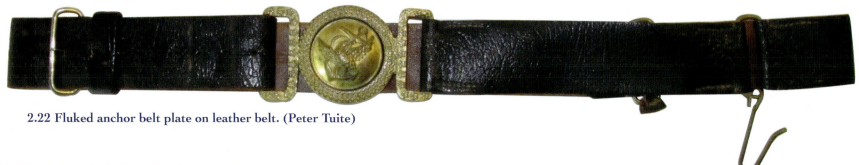

2.22 Fluked anchor belt plate on leather belt. (Peter Tuite)

Navy Lieutenant Alexander B. Pinkham. (Nantucket Historical Association)

2.23 Fluked anchor plate details. (Peter Tuite)

stock pattern.[22] The two pieces are cast and both are match marked *23*.

In the 1820s, interlocking two piece belt plates patterned after the 1819 pattern Army plates with some form of eagle and shield in the center became popular with militia officers.[23] This was also apparently true for naval militia officers. A black leather naval militia belt with an interlocking oval buckle and two connectors with large anchors is shown (2.24). The oval plate tongue (2.25) has an eagle facing its heraldic right with cannon, sun rays, and arms behind, and 13 stars and an *e pluribus unum* banner above.

The wreath section has a single band of oak leaves. The tongue is die struck, while the wreath is cast. This plate is identical to those ascribed to militia officers in the 1830 to 1838 time period.[24] The remainder of the two-inch wide leather belt has two large fouled anchors on round plates with brass chain sword hangers attached. The hook on

2.24 Militia plate and anchor on leather belt. (Peter Tuite)

one of the anchor plates has a serpent head (2.26). David Farragut is seen wearing a very similar belt plate in an 1838 portrait that post-dates the Navy's introduction of its first pattern belt plate in 1830.

A woven blue silk dirk belt with a similar plate design is also shown (2.27). The blue silk belt indicates it was worn by a naval officer. The plate motif on the half shown is the same as that described above, with the eagle facing heraldic left, and the two halves were connected with an S shaped snake clasp (2.28). This plate is die cast. The clasp is the same as that shown in 2.16. This plate is identical to the ones shown on a leather belt described as a sword or dirk belt in O'Donnell.[25] It would appear that this plate design was also a popular one among naval officers during the period. These two militia

2.25 Militia anchor belt plate details. (Peter Tuite)

23

2.26 Militia belt anchor and sword holder

plates are shown together (2.29) for comparison purposes.

The Texas Navy was established in January 1836.[26] Under the command of Charles E. Hawkins (USN 1816-1826), they helped win independence by preventing a Mexican blockade of the Texas coast. In 1839, the Texas Congress acquired six new vessels and placed them under the command of Edwin Moore, then a Lieutenant in the United States Navy. For three years the Texas Navy raided the Mexican coast and kept the Mexican fleet focused on defending its own coastline. When Texas joined the Union in 1846, the Texas Navy was merged into the U.S. Navy. The belt plate shown (2.30) is the only surviving example of the plates worn by officers of the Texas Navy. The design motif is a vertical fouled anchor with a star above surrounded by an oak leaf and acorn wreath with a single tie at its bottom. It is patterned after the 1832 General Staff Officer's plate[27] and was probably made by Ames, since they were a major supplier to the state of Texas after its independence. The plate is gold-

Portrait of David Farragut wearing a militia belt plate. (U.S. Naval Academy Museum)

2.27 Militia blue silk dirk belt. (Peter Tuite)

2.28 Militia belt plate details. (Peter Tuite)

gilded cast silver with a die struck anchor and star and wreath soldered to its face. The rear is indented to accept the tongue.

As evident from the 1838 Farragut portrait and the much later CDV of the old unidentified naval officer, a wide range of belt plate or clasp designs were worn by naval officers through the 1830s and beyond. However, the introduction of belt plate patterns in the 1830 naval regulations would mark the beginning of the end for the artful naval belt plate designs shown above.

2.30 Texas Navy belt plate. (Dr. Allen D. Phillips)

2.29 Comparison of Militia belt plate motifs. (Peter Tuite)

PATTERN 1830 BELTS AND PLATES

The first publication of U.S. Navy uniform regulations was in 1797,[1] and the prescription for buttons was simply: *Buttons, yellow metal, and to have the foul anchor and eagle on the same.* In 1802[2] this was modified to read: *the buttons of yellow metal, with the foul anchor and American eagle, surrounded with 15 stars.* The 1813 uniform regulations were identical, but the 1820[3] regulations made some changes, and four different buttons were prescribed. The order indicates that: *The buttons are to be as described in drawing No. 1.* An article by Captain James Tily,[4] USN, a prominent authority on navy uniforms, indicates that no drawings were available. However, Tily's article states that attached to the order was a typed statement that described the buttons as follows:

3.1 Graphic with 1820 Captain's button

Captain of the Navy - Eagle perched on anchor stock surrounded by 13 stars and looking over his left shoulder. [Button No. 1]

Masters Commandant, Lieutenants Commandant and Lieutenants – Eagle perched on a branch holding a shield with his left wing and looking over his own right shoulder. [Button No. 2]

A sketch of the Captain's button is illustrated (2.1). The 1830[5] regulations extended use of the No. 1 button as follows:

Buttons
The buttons to be worn by all officers, are to be the present pattern for Captains, or what is called No. 1, when small buttons are not specified, the large ones are to be worn.

In 1830, with 615 officers in service, the Navy took the next step in standardizing what officers wore by using patterns (illustrations) to

3.2 Pattern 1820 Button. (Peter Tuite)

define swords, epaulettes, buttons, chapeaus, and belt plates. For belts the regulation simply provided:

Belts
Blue webbing for undress, white webbing for dress, as per pattern.

The pattern was a full size drawing that specifically described the items shown. The pattern for the 1830 belt plate was based on the 1820 No. 1 button design for Captains, which became the button for all officers in 1830. The pattern drawing that accompanied the regulations has not been found by the author, but the corresponding button is shown (3.2).

These first pattern plates, like the button, had an eagle facing its heraldic left on a vertical anchor surrounded by 13 stars, although the number of stars and other features would vary with time. The known variables among the surviving examples include the plate's overall size, the width and design of the wreath that surrounds the tongue, the design of the eagle and its surroundings, and the number of stars that surround the eagle. This chapter examines the belts worn by naval officers with pattern 1830 plates, a range of plates that depict the variables in plate design features as well as methods of plate construction.

Belts that accompany presentation swords are invaluable in determining when the items were made. In 1834, a pattern 1830 sword was presented to William E. McKenney,[6] then a lieutenant on the *USS United States*. The presentation sword was accompanied

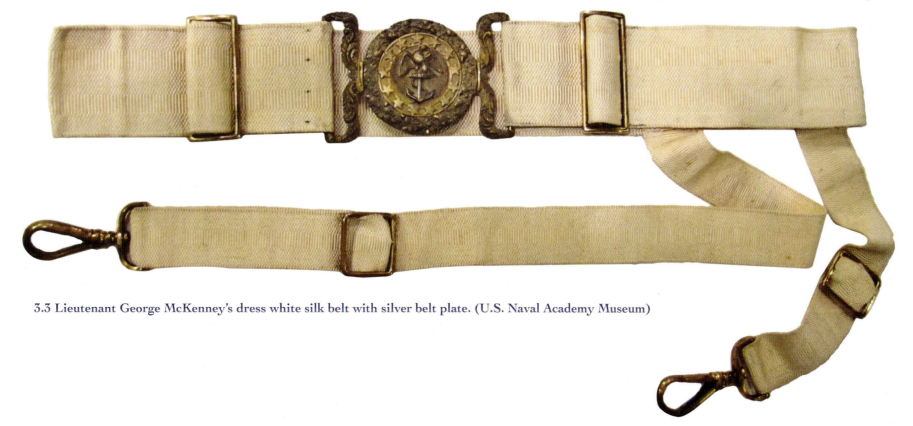

3.3 Lieutenant George McKenney's dress white silk belt with silver belt plate. (U.S. Naval Academy Museum)

3.4 Lieutenant George McKenney's silver belt details. (U.S. Naval Academy Museum)

by an elaborate belt of white linen (3.3). The white linen belt has two rectangular adjustment buckles with four teeth and two sword hangers, with all furniture being silver with gold gilding. The two-piece plate (3.4) is made of presentation grade solid silver with gold gilt. The essentially round, relatively large tongue portion depicts an eagle on a vertical anchor facing its heraldic left surrounded by 13 large stars within a separate ring. The wreath with rectangular cutout is intricately chased with acorns and oak leaves, and the ornate belt loops are chased with florals. The plate is constructed of four cast pieces – three pieces for the tongue and a single casting for the wreath. The tongue pieces are soldered together. The reverse of the tongue is engraved within a rectangle: *H. Bird/Cheapside/London* (inset). The same three silver maker's touch marks are stamped on the tongue and the belt loop.

3.5 Dress blue silk dirk belt and belt plate. (Jack Bethune)

3.6 Early dirk belt plate details. (Jack Bethune)

3. 7 Pattern 1830 plate with 13 stars. (Peter Tuite)

Another fine example of an early plate on a blue silk dirk belt is illustrated in (3.5). Although the plate (3.6) on this dirk belt is relatively small, it closely resembles the button shown above. The eagle is primitive and is on a lined background. The tongue section contains two line motifs: one oval around the eagle surrounded by 13 stars, and one circular around the periphery of the tongue. These motifs are rarely seen on these plates. The wreath is fairly narrow, with oak leaves and berries, and has ties above and below. The belt loops are very ornate. Construction consists of three cast pieces, with the belt loop soldered to the tongue. The back surfaces are japanned, and the tongue cutout in the wreath is regular, with a step to lock the tongue. Both pieces are match marked with the scratched-in Roman numeral *XVII*. This belt is associated with a dirk that appears to have been made in China, where the plate could have also been made.

Not all pattern 1830 plates were as ornate or fine as those described above. A more traditional example of this plate is shown next (3.7). This period eagle, also on a lined background, is surrounded by 13 stars on an oval within a circular tongue. The belt loops are simple, as is the case for most of these plates. The wreath has two diagonal wraps at top and bottom, and the pieces are match marked *18* and *8*. Construction is typical – three cast pieces with the tongue medallion soldered to the belt loop. The wreath is roughly cast with a regular cutout to accept the tongue.

3.8 Silver pattern 1830 plate with 13 stars. (Peter Tuite)

Another example with 13 stars is shown (3.8). Here the eagle is on a lined background within an oval with a rope line motif border. The circular periphery of the tongue also has a rope line motif border. The wreath is relatively narrow, includes the typical laurel leaf and berry motif, and has no wraps. It is constructed of two porous castings, and the wreath has a regular cutout for the tongue. It has been repaired, and a replacement loop has been soldered to the wreath.

Blue silk dress belts also had brass chain sword hangers, and an example is shown (3.9). The belt is continuous, and the chain sword hangers consist of links with plain and rope-like designs. The belt plate (3.10) also differs from those shown above. In this example, the eagle is on a plain oval

3.9 Pattern 1830 belt plate on dress blue silk dress belt with chain hangers. (Jack A. Frost)

3.10 Details of patter belt plate on blue silk dress belt. (Jack A. Frost)

background and both the inner and outer surrounds are plain, instead of depicting a rope motif. The wreath design is composed of oak leaves with berries and ties at its top and bottom. The tongue is die struck and soldered to the belt loop extender, which is also soldered to the belt loop. All other pieces are cast. The back of the wreath has two circular recesses and a notch to accept the tongue.

Two examples with a 17 star eagle surround are also illustrated. The first example shows the plate on a blue silk dress belt (3.11). The plate details are also shown (3.12). The eagle is on a lined background surrounded by 17 stars within the oval. The wreath has the leaf and berry motif with opposing diagonal

ties at top and bottom. The pieces are match marked *18*. It is constructed of three pieces, with the die struck tongue medallion soldered to the belt loop section. The tongue section is recessed to accept the wreath, and the wreath has a regular cutout and recesses to accept the tongue. The entire back surface is japanned.

The other example with 17 stars (3.13) also shows the eagle on the typical lined background within a distinctly raised oval within the circle. The wreath has the typical oak leaf and berry motif, and unlike the one above has crossed wraps at top and bottom. The pieces are match marked *46*, which

3.11 Pattern 1830 belt plate on dress blue silk belt. (Jack Bethune)

31

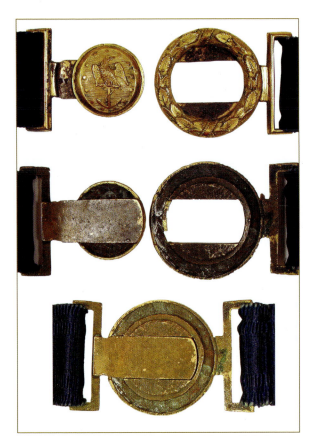

3.12 Detail of belt plate on dress blue silk belt. (Jack Bethune)

3.13 Pattern 1830 belt plate with 17 stars. (Peter Tuite)

3.14 Undress leather belt with 17 star pattern 1830 belt plate. (Jack A. Frost)

3.15 Details of Pattern 1830 belt plate on leather undress belt. (Jack A. Frost)

3.16 Undress leather belt with Pattern 1830 belt plate by Ames. (Peter Tuite)

could indicate a popular design. The tongue medallion is die struck and soldered to the belt loop. The wreath has a regular cutout and the castings are smooth.

The last example is on a black leather undress belt with leather hangers (3.14). Like the one above, this belt plate (3.15) has 17 stars, but on a plain background and without rope motifs on either the oval or circular surround. The wreath consists of oak leaves without berries, with ties at its top and bottom. Both pieces are match marked *104,* and the wreath also has a *7.* All pieces are cast except the tongue, which is die struck. The belt loop extender is soldered to the belt loop and the tongue. There is a single deep recess around the periphery of the wreath and a notch to accept the tongue.

Two examples of plates with 26 star eagle surrounds are shown. The first example was supplied by Ames and is on a plain black leather belt (3.16). The belt plate (3.17) is deeply chased and has a relatively large eagle on a stippled background. There are no rope line motifs around the oval containing the

3.17 Details of Ames Pattern 1830 belt plate. (Peter Tuite)

motifs on the periphery of the oval or the tongue. The wreath has the Ames oak leaf and acorn motif, and has two crossed wraps at its top and bottom, which may suggest it is later than the Ames plate. It is well made, with the die struck medallion soldered to the cast belt loop and the wreath being cast. Both the tongue section and the wreath section have recesses to accept the other piece. Match markings consist of six hash marks at the outside of both belt loops. The back of the cast wreath is flat and the entire rear surface has been japanned.

The next two examples of pattern plates are on belts that belonged to Thomas Brownell[7] (USN 1812-1818, 1840-1867). Although he served during the War of 1812, he resigned in 1818, then returned to the Navy as Master in October 1840 and finally

eagle, nor around the 26 stars within the tongue oval. The wreath has the oak leaf and acorn motif that Ames would use for its 1852 plates, and has crossed wraps at its top and bottom. Both the tongue and wreath are match marked *550* on their front faces. It is doubtful that 550 of these plates were made. The tongue has the circular cutout to fit the wreath. The plate is constructed of 5 pieces – medallion soldered to the belt loop extension, which is soldered to the belt loop, and the wreath soldered to the belt loop. The tongue medallion is die struck and the other pieces are cast. The backs of all pieces are japanned.

The second example with 26 stars (3.18) is somewhat unique, in that its wreath extends beyond the belt loops – a feature we see later in some pattern 1841 and pattern 1852 belt plates. The eagle is on a lightly stippled background and, like the Ames plate above, there are no line

3.18 Pattern 1830 belt plate with 26 stars. (Peter Tuite)

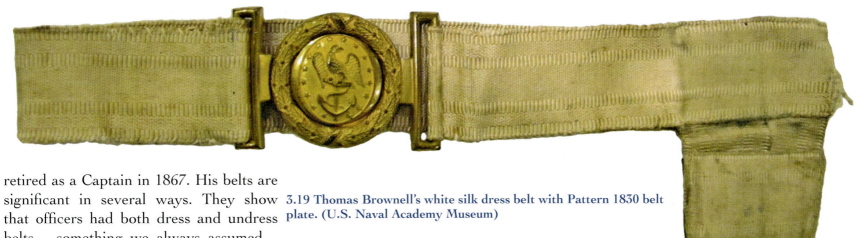

retired as a Captain in 1867. His belts are significant in several ways. They show that officers had both dress and undress belts – something we always assumed – and that belts with frogs were being worn in 1840. More importantly, his belts are representative of the types of pattern 1830 plates that were being sold in late 1840.

3.19 Thomas Brownell's white silk dress belt with Pattern 1830 belt plate. (U.S. Naval Academy Museum)

The first example is his dress white silk belt (3.19) with a frog, as distinguished from the William McKenney dress belt shown in 3.3. The plate details are shown separately (3.20). Although match marked *6* on the tongue, this plate is essentially the same as that match marked *46* shown on plate 3.12.

The second example is his undress black leather belt (3.21) with frog attachment. This belt is fine leather with a linen backing, as opposed to the plain leather belt shown in 3.16 and stamped Ames. Again, the belt plate is shown separately (3.22). This plate has the 13 star surround with eagle on a lined background. The wreath is also similar to those shown previously, and the tongue has a circular cutout to accept the wreath. Plate construction is different from the others shown. This plate

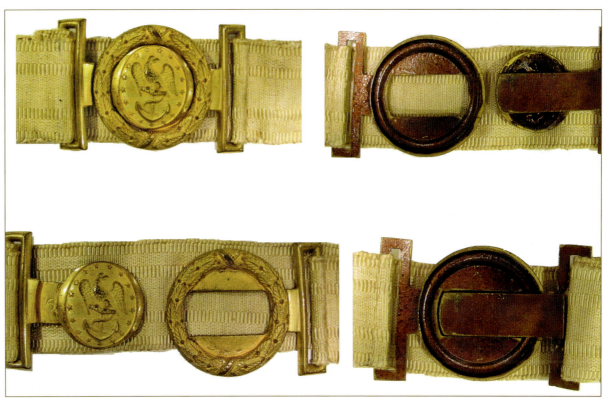

3.20 Details of Thomas Brownell's Pattern 1830 belt plate on dress belt. (U.S. Naval Academy Museum)

3.21 Thomas Brownell's leather undress belt with Pattern 1830 belt plate. (U.S. Naval Academy Museum)

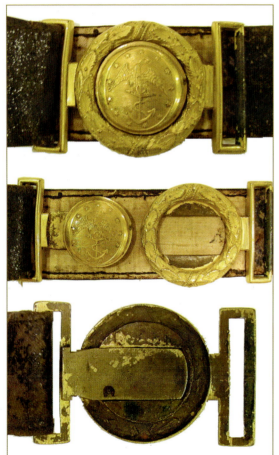

3.22 Thomas Brownell plate on undress belt. (U.S. Naval Academy Museum)

is comprised of four separate pieces and all pieces are cast. The tongue consists of three of these pieces, with the center medallion soldered to the tongue extension and the tongue extension soldered to the belt loop. This plate indicates that 13 star plates – the original pattern – were still being sold in late 1840.

The last example shown (3.23) could well be the latest example known, for it contains 27 stars in the eagle surround. The plate is deeply chased, with the eagle on a stippled background and, as with the other relatively late plates, there are no line motifs. The wreath has the oak leaf and acorn motif with crossed wraps at top and bottom. The pieces are match marked with a deeply stamped *HHH* on the inside surface of the wreath and an inverted *NNN* on the tongue extension to the belt loop. The wreath cutout for the tongue is relatively wide, and there is a recess to accept the tongue. All three pieces are cast, and the tongue medallion is soldered to the belt loop extension. The rear cast surfaces

Passed Midshipman Arthur Sinclair wearing Pattern 1830 belt plate. (U.S. Naval Academy Museum)

Sinclair Belt Plate Detail. (U.S. Naval Academy Museum)

are smooth and the entire back has been japanned.

In the absence of presentations like the McKenney plate above or the Brownell plates, it is difficult to date these plates. The Brownell plates are the most relevant

3.23 Late Pattern 1830 plate with 27 stars. (Jack Bethune)

to dating, and show that both 13 and 17 star plates were being purchased in late 1840. The Ames belt is also important, since Ames did not make belt plates until at least 1837, making the Ames plate relatively late. Additionally, since the Ames plate has the oak leaf and acorn motif that would become its trademark on later plates, it is reasonable to assume that the other plates with this wreath motif post date the Ames plate.

The pattern for the 1830 belt plate was the first one used by the Navy, but like the pattern 1830 swords, manufacturers took liberties with the plate design and construction details. Three typical pattern 1830 belt plates are shown together (3.24) to illustrate the range of variables among these plate designs.

3.24 Comparison of three different Pattern 1830 plates. (Peter Tuite)

Chapter

4

PATTERN 1841 BELTS AND PLATES

During the 11 years since the Navy issued its first set of uniform regulations with pattern drawings, the size of the Navy only increased by about 325 officers, to about 940. As seen in chapter three, the numbers of surviving pattern 1830 belts and plates is relatively large, but this is not the case for the belts and plates that came to be known as the pattern 1841 plates.

The Navy's 1841 Uniform Regulations[1] were published on 19 February 1841 and provided more extensive descriptions for belts than the earlier one:

Belts for undress to be of black leather, mountings to be of yellow gilt: for full dress the belts to be of white webbing, both to be 1-1/2 inch wide; the mountings to be of yellow gilt. …. and the mountings of the belt, to be according to pattern.

4.1 1841 Pattern belt plate drawing from 1841 Uniform Regulatinos

Buttons of full size

4.2 1841 Pattern button drawing from 1841 Uniform Regulations

The pattern drawing for the 1841 belt plate (4.1) and the corresponding buttons (4.2) are illustrated at the size presented on the pattern drawing. As shown on the drawing, the eagle is sitting on an upright fouled anchor looking over to its heraldic left and surrounded by 13 stars. Thus, the eagle on anchor motif is identical to that for the pattern 1830 belt plates. For this new pattern, the 1830 oval surround with laurel leaf wreath has been replaced with a circular surround with an oak leaf and acorn wreath. This pattern represented very little change to what was being worn by Navy officers since 1830.

4.3 Comparison of Pattern 1830 and 1841 belt plates. (Peter Tuite)

Based on the author's observations, it is not clear that a belt plate that complied with this pattern drawing (i.e., eagle facing the heraldic left) was ever manufactured. That is not so surprising when you look at the similarity between the two patterns. Instead, the belt plate typically referred to as the "pattern 1841" plate has the eagle facing its heraldic right, just the opposite shown in the pattern drawing. It also appears that some of the early plates retained the oval border on the tongue containing the eagle. What is believed to be an early pattern 1841 belt plate is compared to a typical pattern 1830 belt plate (4.3), with the pattern 1841 plate at the top. This plate was made by Ames and is so marked (see below).

It is very unusual, because the tongue is inserted into the wreath from the wearer's left side, while every other two-piece belt plate discussed in this book has the tongue inserted into the wreath from the wearer's right side, as would be typical for someone who is right handed. It is doubtful that Ames made a special belt plate for a left-handed officer.

The details of the Ames manufactured plate are shown next (4.4). The inside of the wreath is stamped *N.P. Ames / Cabotville / Mass.*, but the *N.P. Ames* is upside down relative to the other stampings. Unlike the 1830 eagles, a shield has been added, but the eagle still sits within an oval and is surrounded by 13 stars on a stippled background. All of the 1841

plates observed by the author have the 13-star surround, as opposed to the variable numbers of stars seen on the 1830 belt plates. The tongue is cast and soldered to the belt loop with its extension for insertion into the wreath. The wreath is adorned with two sprigs of oak leaves tied at the bottom, but unlike the Ames plate in chapter two and the above pattern drawing, there are no acorns. The wreath is cast, has a rectangular cutout with rounded ends, and has a circular recess inside its periphery. The belt loops are unadorned and the back is japanned. The location of Cabotville would date this plate after 1845.

The next example illustrated (4.5) is an earlier version of this belt plate, and except for the eagle's direction is closer to the 1841 pattern drawing than any of the others observed. The eagle sits on a slightly slanted anchor with uplifted head and does not have a shield on

4.4 Ames Pattern 1841 belt plate. (Peter Tuite)

its breast. The surround is circular with a rope border and the background is plain. The wreath has an oak leaf and acorn design with a single cross tie at its bottom. All the parts are cast, with the tongue soldered to the belt loop extension, and the tongue cutout is wider than that on the Ames plate above. There is a slight recess on the belt loop extension to accommodate the wreath. Like the Ames plate, there is a recess inside the wreath periphery. There is no japanning.

In 1832, the Royal Navy prescribed two-piece belt plates for its officers that had: *gilt mountings with circular fronts, two inches diameter, laurel embossed edges, crown and anchor in the center.*[2] Plates for admirals had the crown and anchor and laurel in the center. There are numerous images of Royal Navy officers wearing these laurel wreath belt plates,[3] and an example that was recently auctioned

4.5 Early Pattern 1841 belt plate. (Peter Tuite)

4.6 Laurel wreath Pattern 1841 belt plate on leather. (Jack Bethune)

4.7 Laurel wreath Pattern 1841 belt plate details. (Jack Bethune)

shows the design to consist of an overlapping laurel wreath with berries with ties at the top and bottom.[4] Thus, the overlapping laurel wreath was in use by the Royal Navy as early as 1832, and the laurel wreath design of the pattern 1841 plate discussed below was undoubtedly based on the Royal Navy laurel wreath. It appears that belt plates of this style were very popular with U.S. Navy officers, and they represent most of the pattern 1841 plates observed by the author.

An example of one of these plates on leather is shown next (4.6). The undress black leather belt has chain sword slings attached to the belt by brass loops. This plate design (4.7) differs significantly from the plates shown above. The eagle with shield sits on a relatively large vertical fouled anchor surrounded by 13 stars. Note that the tongue has no border and the background is plain. The wreath consists of a laurel leaf and berry array with a single tie at its bottom and extends beyond the plain belt loops. It has a rectangular cutout with rounded ends, and both the wreath and the tongue are stamped 5. The tongue is stamped and soldered to the belt loop extension and the wreath is cast. There is a slight recess in the back of the wreath to accept the tongue and the remainder of the wreath back surface is flat.

This is the most prevalent design observed for pattern 1841 belt plates, and except for slight differences in the eagle's wings, the details of the line fouling the anchor, and plate construction details, the plates described below have essentially the same basic design.

The next belt plate (4.8) shows missing gilding, where excess soldering flux occasionally overflowed onto the front of the tongue during assembly, and the tongue motif differs slightly from the one on the left. The most noticeable differences are the slanted anchor and the smooth, as opposed to lined, surface of the fouled line. The wreath design motifs are unchanged, and this was observed on all these plates. Plate construction differs, as there is a recess around the wreath periphery and another recess to ensure that the back is flat when the tongue is inserted into the wreath.

Another very fine example of this belt plate on leather is shown (4.9). The undress black belt is white buff on the inside and the plate and elaborate chain sword slings are highly gilded. Like the belt above, the slings are attached to the belt with loops, but these loops are elongated as opposed to circular. Again, we find the same basic design of the tongue and wreath

(4.10), with the tongue background stippled as opposed to plain and finer chasing in both the tongue and wreath, with both pieces match marked *12*. Plate construction is essentially the same as that immediately preceeding, but the flat back of the plate is polished, which is indicative of its higher quality.

Contrast the fine belt plate on leather in figure 4.10 to the next belt plate shown (4.11), where the casting is relatively crude. The tongue motif is the same as that shown above (4.8), as is the wreath motif. While the tongue is cast, other details of its construction are the same as the referenced one above, except that the back surfaces are japanned.

Another example of this design on a fine lined undress black leather segmented belt is shown (4.12). The belt connecting loops are relatively large, and are used for attachment of the leather sword belt slings. The belt plate design (4.13) is similar to those discussed above. The tongue is die struck, and the remaining pieces are cast. Like two of the

4.8 Another laurel Pattern 1841 belt plate. (Jack Bethune)

others shown, the back of the wreath is flat, as opposed to having a recess, and there is a notch for mating with the tongue. The two pieces are match marked with a *2* on the tongue and a *5* on the inside of the wreath.

The author owns an identical plate with the pieces match marked *90*, indicating that this particular manufacturer supplied many such plates.

4.9 Laurel wreath Pattern 1841 belt plate on leather. (John A. Gunderson)

4.10 Laurel wreath Pattern 1841 belt plate details. (John A. Gunderson)

It appears that in actual practice, the basic pattern 1841 belt plate consists of a large laurel and berry wreath surrounding an inner circular tongue without border but encircled by 13 stars, all centering an eagle with shield on its breast facing its heraldic *right*, rather than to the *left* as shown in the original pattern drawing, and perched on a vertical anchor. Despite this variance from the pattern drawing, the numbers extant indicate widespread use by naval officers. As noted above, the overlapping laurel and berry wreath was adopted from the Royal Navy, and it appears that the tongue design was adopted from a Navy button of the period. In the late 1830s and 1840s,[5] U.S. naval officers were wearing buttons with the eagle facing its heraldic right. As illustrated (4.14), this button design is identical to that on the tongue of these belt plates. The question is, when were these belt plates made? It was almost certainly after the early belt plate shown previously (4.5), but whether or not they predate the Ames post-1845 plate (4.4) is unknown. Another unknown is the place of manufacture, as they are all unmarked, except for the bench marks. They could easily have been manufactured in England, where the wreaths were abundant, or assembled in the U.S. with imported wreaths and a U.S. Navy button based tongue design. More research is needed to answer these questions.

4.11 Laurel wreath Pattern 1841 belt plate details. (John A. Gunderson)

4.12 Laurel wreath Pattern 1841 belt plate on segmented leather belt. (Jack A. Frost)

4.13 Laurel wreath Pattern 1841 belt plate details. (Jack A. Frost)

4. 14 c1835-1852 naval officer's button. (Peter Tuite)

This design is compared to what could only be considered variants (4.15). As shown, the *de facto* 1841 belt plate bears no resemblance to the Ames plate, nor to the one that pre-dated the Ames plate.

4.15 Comparison of early Pattern 1841 belt plates and typical laurel wreath belt plate. (Peter Tuite)

Chapter 5

PATTERN 1852 BELTS AND PLATES

On 8 March 1852, the Secretary of the Navy issued a new set of uniform regulations[1] that provided the following guidelines for naval officer's belts:

*Shall be of plain black glazed leather, not less than one inch and a half, nor more than two inches wide, with slings of the same not less than one-half nor more than three-quarters of an inch wide, and a hook in the forward ring to suspend the sword. Belt-plate of yellow gilt in front, two inches in diameter, **as per pattern**.*

The referenced belt pattern as originally issued, full size and in color, is illustrated (5.1). The Navy used the same design motif until 1941, when it changed the direction the eagle was facing from heraldic left to heraldic right.

5.1 1852 regulation pattern 1852 belt plate graphic

There are numerous examples of these plates available due to the length of their use and the numbers of officers wearing them over a period of about 95 years. This chapter examines the two piece plates and belts worn, in some cases through the twentieth century, as well as the false two piece (one piece) plates worn from the

latter part of the nineteenth century through 1945, although little changed after about 1913. This period where naval officers wore one piece plates is typified by the fairly elaborate dress belts that were worn to distinguish rank, and many of these belts are also illustrated

In early April 1852, the Navy ordered 500 officer swords from Ames.[2] The order included scabbards, belts, and buckles at a total cost of $22.50 per sword, and was to be delivered to the Navy Yards at Boston, New York, Philadelphia, Washington, and Norfolk in quantities specified by the original order. Ames delivered 420 swords by 10 December 1852, and the final 80 were delivered to the New York Naval Yard on 5 January 1853. These inspected swords and belts, by definition, conformed to the regulations and the pattern.

The pattern belt plate supplied by Ames under its U.S. Navy contract is illustrated (5.2).

5.2 Inspected 1852 plate by Ames. (Peter Tuite)

As shown, it is stamped *P* above *R.B.H.*, where P is the proof mark and RBH are the initials of Commander Robert B. Hitchcock, the Navy inspector.[3] There is evidence that most if not all of the swords contained inspector's marks, but it is not clear that belt plates were similarly inspected, as few inspected plates are extant. Another Ames manufactured plate belonging to Vice-Admiral Stephen Rowan (USN 1826-1889)[4] is also shown on leather (5.3). Since Rowan was a prominent naval officer in 1852 it is likely that he received one of the original Ames swords and belts, but his belt plate is unmarked.

When the 1852 regulations were issued the Navy had relatively few officers (about 1,460, including about 400 midshipmen).[5]

Rear Admiral Andrew Foote (1806-1863) wearing Pattern 1852 Large Wreath Belt Plate.

5.3 Vice Admiral Stephen Rowan's 1852 plate by Ames on leather. (Peter Tuite)

When the Civil War began in 1861, naval officer strength was only slightly higher at about 1,550 men, with about 370 of these officers choosing to join the South.[6] The Civil War would increase the number of naval officers considerably. By the war's end in 1865 there were about 6,700 naval officers in service. Thus, there were relatively large numbers of pattern 1852 plates made during the war. Moreover, some of the two piece designs of pattern 1852 plates were used

5.4 Pattern 1852 plate with slant anchor. (Dr. Allen D. Phillips)

through the early twentieth century, thus increasing their numbers.

The large number of plates made and the number of manufacturers leads to wide variability in the design features of pattern 1852 plates. These variances relative to the *de facto* pattern by Ames are discussed. When looking at the tongue design, the variables include the location of the 13 stars relative to the anchor, the size of the stars, the orientation of the eagle's head, the orientation of the anchor, and the design of the rope surround. The features of the Ames plate include two stars below the anchor, large stars, an eagle

looking straight ahead, an anchor slanted up, and a heavily chased rope surround.

When looking at the wreath, the variables include its size, its position relative to the belt loops, the number and design of the ties, the presence or absence of acorns, and the presence or absence of berries. The features of the Ames plate include an oak leaf wreath that does not touch the loops, four ties at 90 degree intervals around the wreath, and relatively large acorns. The belt loop features also vary in terms of their configuration, i.e., square versus rounded corners, their thickness, whether or not there

is a design motif, and the design motif itself. The belt loops on the Ames plates are very distinctive: there is a leaf motif in a triangle at each corner and the members themselves are two different thicknesses.

The rear of the plates also varies. For the tongue, the variances include the method of medallion manufacture (stamped versus cast) and the method, if any, used to attach the medallion to the tongue. For the Ames plate, the tongue and medallion are cast and the medallion is soldered to the tongue. As shown later, some later plates are cast in a single piece. As a general rule, the backs of Ames plates are japanned.

For the back of the wreath the variances include the configuration of the tongue cutout, the outer circumference configuration (round versus irregular), and whether the wreath is flat or recessed. For the Ames plate, the cutout is rectangular with circular sides, the circumference is regular, and there is a recess around the periphery of the wreath.

This chapter will illustrate pattern 1852 plates with different designs manufactured over a span of about 50 years by different manufacturers. The Ames plate used for the above comparisons was the first of its kind, and things changed due to increased demand, changes in manufacturing methods, and economics.

Examples of the variability of these pattern plates are illustrated. The first example (5.4) is a typical pattern plate with the eagle on a slant anchor, its head below the ring of stars, with one star below the

anchor. The oak leaf with acorn wreath is a flat back casting with a crack line. It has an irregular periphery and a regular cutout with small semicircles. It is constructed of three cast pieces, with the medallion soldered to the belt loop extension. The belt loops are adorned with irregular floral motifs.

The next example (5.5) looks similar but is a different plate. Here the eagle is on a horizontal anchor with its head through the ring of stars with no stars below the anchor. The wreath design is similar to that above, but its details differ. The wreath outer periphery is smooth, the circular casting is recessed, and the cutout for the tongue is a simple rectangle. It is also constructed of three cast pieces. The belt loops are adorned with floral motifs.

Another example with a horizontal anchor (5.6) is deeply chased relative to the others above. Here, the eagle has its head through the ring of stars with one star below the anchor. This cast wreath has a flat back with relatively large semicircles in the tongue cutout, and it has an irregular periphery. The medallion is die struck, but since the pieces are mismatched this feature is just an example of the variability in the design and construction of these plates. Again, the belt loops are adorned with floral motifs.

The next example is on leather (5.7) and has the slant anchor like Plate 5.4 above, with one star below the anchor and the eagle head through the ring of stars. The wreath motif includes somewhat larger oak leaves and its periphery is smooth (5.8). It has a rectangular cut out for the tongue. Both

5.5 Pattern 1852 plate with horizontal anchor. (Dr. Allen D. Phillips)

5.6 Pattern 1852 plate - deeply chased. (Dr. Allen D. Phillips)

5.7 Pattern 1852 plate with large oak leaves on leather. (Peter Tuite)

5.8 Pattern 1852 plate with large oak leaves details. (Peter Tuite)

the tongue and the wreath are cast, with the wreath having a recessed back and the tongue having a flat back – a new feature relative to those shown above. The belt loops are adorned with floral motifs like the others.

The next two plates are also different from those above. The first one (5.9) has the horizontal anchor with one star below and the eagle head above the stars. The wreath is

cast with a rectangular cutout with the large semicircles and is notched to fit the tongue. The backs of the wreath and tongue are flat, and the belt loops have symmetrical floral motifs. The second example (5.10) has a steeply slanted anchor, like the Ames plates, with all thirteen stars above the eagle's head. The wreath has relatively large oak leaves and is smooth around its periphery. The wreath and loop extension are cast, and the medallion is die struck and soldered to the belt loop extension. The circular wreath casting is recessed. The belt loops have irregular floral motifs.

Another example on leather (5.11) includes a plate with a very dark patina. The

belt plate (5.12) has the eagle on a slanted anchor with no stars below and the eagle's head extended through the ring of stars. Its construction is very different from the others shown. All pieces are cast, but the belt loop is attached to the side of the medallion instead of across it and the medallion back is a circular recess. The wreath periphery is smooth and has the recess around the circle. The cutout is rectangular, but notched at one end to accept the tongue. The belt loops are adorned like the others.

The next example is on the presentation grade belt (5.13), and is probably the finest example of an 1852 pattern plate extant. The belt is made of high grade leather with

5.9 Pattern 1852 plate with horizontal anchor. (Peter Tuite)

5.10 Pattern 1852 plate with steep slanted anchor. (Peter Tuite)

hand tooled. The tongue was also cast, and the belt loop extension is attached to the medallion at its periphery like the example in 5.12. The belt loops are also unusual, in that they are round as opposed to flat, have rounded ends, and include a rope motif on their surfaces.

Another example on a lieutenant's or ensign's dress belt[7] with its three gold stripes (5.15) post-dates 1869. The belt plate (5.16) is similar to those described above, but like all the others shown it has some different features. The eagle is on a slanted anchor with one star below and its head extends through the array of

5.11 Pattern 1852 plate with dark patina on leather. (Peter Tuite)

red stitching and a support piece for the sword. The belt plate (5.14) is very large, and is made of gold or highly gilded silver. The tongue portion of the plate has the eagle on a horizontal anchor with no stars below and the eagle's head is below the thirteen stars – a typical pattern 1852 plate design. The wreath bears no resemblance to any other known plate. Instead of the acorn and oak leaf motif, it has a circular stand of arms that includes crossed cannon at its top, a crossed cannon and bugle at its bottom, and sea serpents at its sides. The wreath has a recessed irregular cutout for the tongue, and while the back is flat, indicating it was cast, the front is deeply chased, indicating it was

5.12. Pattern 1852 plate with dark patina. (Peter Tuite)

5.13 Presentation grade belt with ornate 1852 belt plate. (U.S. Naval Academy Museum)

stars. The wreath and tongue are cast, but the tongue is cast in one piece. The wreath periphery is smooth, has a rectangular cutout for the tongue, and the circular portion is recessed. The wreath back is stamped above and below the cutout with an *I* and a *C*, which could indicate the maker.

An Admiral's dress belt with the three ¼ inch wide gold stripes prescribed for Rear Admirals and Commodores in the 1883 regulations[8] is shown next (5.17). The belt plate has design motifs similar to those already shown, but the method of construction differs (5.18). The eagle sits on a slanted anchor with one star below, and the eagle's head is through the array of stars. Both tongue and wreath are cast, with the wreath having a flat back and the tongue having a recessed back like that shown in 5.12. The

5.14 Presentation grade ornate 1852 belt plate. (U.S. Naval Academy Museum)

5.15 Pattern 1852 belt plate on Ensign/Lieutenant JG dress belt. (Peter Tuite)

major distinction from those shown before, aside from the belt, is the irregular shaped three part cut out in the wreath to accept the tongue.

As described above, these plates were manufactured and worn from 1852 through 1883 as a minimum. As discussed below, other styles of two piece pattern 1852 plates were worn through the early part of the twentieth century.

There is a group of 1852 pattern plates that have been referred to as "Admirals' Plates" by at least one author. The "c1865" image of Rear Admiral Joseph Skerrett in his Commodore uniform wearing this plate is used to validate this assumption.[9] Skerrett

5.16 Ensign/Lieutenant JG belt plate details. (Peter Tuite)

53

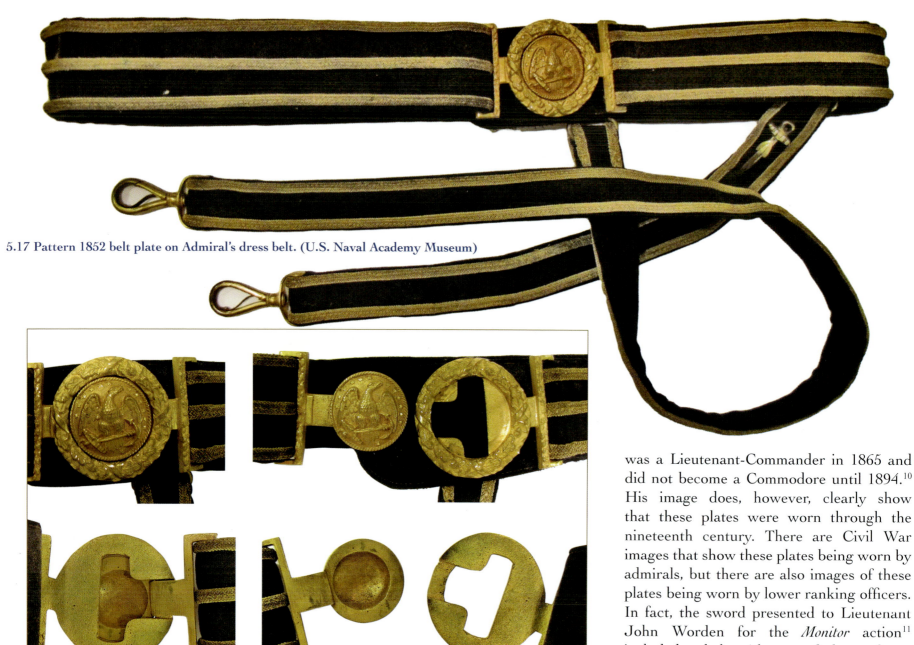

5.17 Pattern 1852 belt plate on Admiral's dress belt. (U.S. Naval Academy Museum)

5.18 Admiral's belt plate details. (U.S. Naval Academy Museum)

was a Lieutenant-Commander in 1865 and did not become a Commodore until 1894.[10] His image does, however, clearly show that these plates were worn through the nineteenth century. There are Civil War images that show these plates being worn by admirals, but there are also images of these plates being worn by lower ranking officers. In fact, the sword presented to Lieutenant John Worden for the *Monitor* action[11] included a belt with one of these plates. Thus, there is no basis for this distinction. This group of plates is distinguished by an

5.19 Comparison of large wreath belt plate to Ames pattern belt plate. (Peter Tuite)

5.20 Dated Pattern 1852 large wreath belt plate. (Jack Bethune)

enlarged wreath that touches the belt loops, but the motifs on both the wreath and the tongue are identical to the pattern motifs. The eagle is on a horizontal anchor with all thirteen stars above. When compared to the original Ames pattern plate (5.19) the differences are readily apparent.

Several examples of these types of pattern 1852 plates are illustrated below. The first plate shown (5.20) is unique because its belt loop is stamped *E.J PAT. 1860 USN*. Thus, these plates were in use before the Civil War. This plate has a cast wreath and a die struck tongue medallion soldered to the belt loop extension. The wreath periphery is smooth

and the cutout for the tongue is rectangular, with a notch to fit the tongue. Note that the rank of admiral did not exist in 1860, so these could hardly be "admiral" plates.[12]

The next plate shown (5.21), with both pieces match marked *19*, is essentially identical to the one above. The detail is not as fine, nor is the fit between the wreath and tongue. Both of the above plates have japanned backs.

The belt that accompanied the sword given to Lieutenant John Worden for the CSS *Virginia* and USS *Monitor* action in 1862 is shown (5.22) . The sword was made by Tiffany, so it can be assumed that Tiffany also

supplied the belt, although it is unmarked. The belt, with acorns and gold stripes, is very similar to that prescribed for Admirals in the 1869 uniform regulations.[13] Although heavily gilded with the design motif well defined (5.23), this plate is similar in design and construction to those described above.

Another plate on a leather belt is typical (5.24). While the design is almost identical to those above (5.25), the methods of construction differ. This plate consists of two cast pieces with an irregular wreath and a different wreath cutout for the tongue.

Leather belt styles differed, and another plate on leather is also shown (5.26). The

face of this plate was manufactured with a finer casting than the one shown on page 58 (5.27), and its construction is consistent with the first three shown.

From the five examples presented above, it is clear that the design motif on these plates did not vary – the only variance is the depth of chasing, or more appropriately, the level of detail in the casting used by the manufacturer. The construction details are also similar: four of the five have a die struck tongue with cast loop extension and wreath, a smooth wreath outer periphery, and a symmetrical wreath cutout for the tongue. All four are japanned. The other one shown (5.25) is constructed of two cast pieces, has an irregular wreath outer periphery, and a different wreath cutout for the tongue. It is not japanned. Two of the five are also dated,

5.21 Large wreath Pattern 1852 belt plate. (Peter Tuite)

5.22 Dress belt presented to Lieutenant John Worden with large wreath Pattern 1852 belt plate. (U.S. Naval Academy Museum)

5.23 Details of John Worden belt plate. (U.S. Naval Academy Museum)

with the first made in 1860 before the Civil War and the plate on the Worden belt made during the Civil War. The plate shown in 5.25 could have post-dated the Civil War, but it may also be a lower quality plate produced during the war. From the image of Rear Admiral Skerrett noted above, these plates were also worn through the latter part of the nineteenth century, and on their face they were essentially all the same.

The uniform regulations of 1852 were modified in 1862,[14] 1864,[15] and 1866,[16] but these new regulations did not change the pattern. In fact, the 1866 regulations repeated the pattern graphic in the 1852 regulations (5.28).

5.25 Details of large wreath belt plate. (Peter Tuite)

5.24 Large Wreath Pattern 1852 Belt Plate on Leather. (Peter Tuite)

The Civil War demand for belts also led to the introduction of another variant to the Ames 1852 plate shown above (5.2). This variant has the same tongue design as the earlier 1852 plates, but the details of the wreath are simplified: the leaves are laurel instead of oak and contain berries instead of acorns. At least one author refers to this plate design as the "general service" plate, and infers its use pre-dates the release of the 1852 regulations.[17] There is no objective evidence to support the designation of "general service" or its use before the Civil War. They are not illustrated in the 1862, 1864, or 1866 uniform regulation, nor any Navy orders during this period. The design is, however, shown as a "navy belt plate" in the 1864 Schuyler Hartley and Graham catalogue[18] (5.29). Note that this graphic is illustrated in the Army section of the catalogue – an obvious error in printing. A

5.27 Details of finely chased large wreath belt plate. (Peter Tuite)

comparison of one of these plates to the Ames pattern 1852 plate illustrates the differences between them (5.30).

The major distinguishing features of these 1852 pattern plates are their size and simplified laurel wreath. The diameter is

5.28 1866 regulation Pattern 1852 plate graphic

No. 53.

Gilt Eagle Plate.

5.29 1864 Schuyler Hartley and Graham navy plate graphic.

5.30 Comparison of Ames pattern 1852 and laurel wreath Pattern 1852 belt plates. (Peter Tuite)

larger, and the wreath is wider; it overlaps unadorned belt loops, has a single tie at its bottom, and contains berries instead of the acorns found on the earlier plates. The tongue design is also unique unto itself. All thirteen stars are above the eagle, the anchor is almost horizontal with a slight downward inclination, and the eagle's head is below the circle of stars. This same wreath design was used for Civil War vintage Revenue Marine plates (5.31) and on some large pattern 1841 plates (5.32). Like the other large plates discussed above, there is no variability in the designs on the face of these plates manufactured in the U.S., but their construction details differ.

The first example shown is an early well-constructed version of this plate (5.33). This plate is japanned, and has the rectangular cutout in the wreath associated with other early plates shown previously. The tongue medallion is cast, but it is made of three pieces: two for the tongue and one for the wreath.

Another example of this style plate is on a black presentation grade belt (5.34) that accompanied the sword given to George Morris (USN 1852-1875)[19] for his gallantry during the action between the CSS *Virginia* and the USS *Cumberland* at Hampton Roads on 8 March 1862. The sword was supplied by Horstmann.[20] As shown (5.35), although heavily gilded, the tongue and wreath designs are identical to the plates shown above. The wreath has a circular cutout with two small notches and one large notch for the tongue, and its periphery is irregular. Both the tongue and wreath are cast with recessed backs and match marked *38*.

Another example of an undress leather belt is shown (5.36). The designs on the

5.31 Comparison of Laurel Wreath Plate to Civil War Vintage Revenue Marine Belt Plate. (Peter Tuite)

5.32 Comparison of Laurel Wreath Plate to Pattern 1841 Belt Plate. (Peter Tuite)

wreath and tongue (5.37) are identical to other U.S. made plates, but the construction is relatively crude, possibly suggesting earlier manufacture. Both pieces are rough castings with the tongue and wreath recessed. The wreath is irregular around its periphery, and while the cutout has the typical three notches for the tongue, they are relatively rough. The tongue is marked *63* on its face.

This plate style was also made in England, and one stamped *Joseph Starkey / 23 Conduit St./London* on the front of the wreath recess is illustrated (5.38). The design motifs on the wreath and tongue are different than U.S. made plates. It has a thinner cast wreath. It also has much deeper chasing than the others shown, which is indicative of its finer quality. The construction of this plate is also completely different. This plate has a

stamped medallion soldered to the tongue, and the wreath has a rectangular cutout with rounded ends like those on the earlier 1852 plates shown above. The wreath periphery is irregular. Starkey was at this address from 1856, so this plate could pre-date the Civil War, although this is doubtful.[21]

A probable Civil War period plate on leather is shown (5.39). Although cast in two pieces with an articulated cutout, the

Lt. Cdr William G. Saltonstall wearing Pattern 1852 Belt Plate. (USN)

5.33 Early Pattern 1852 laurel wreath belt plate with japanned back. (Peter Tuite)

5.34 George Morris presentation grade belt with laurel wreath belt plate. (U.S. Naval Academy Museum)

5.35 Details of George Morris belt plate. (U.S. Naval Academy Museum)

castings are rough and the cutout is irregular, indicating relatively early manufacture. Like the plate described earlier (5.16), the back of the wreath is stamped with an *I* above the cutout and a *C* below the cutout. Contrast this to the next plate of this type, where the castings are well done and the cutout is symmetrical. This plate is undoubtedly of later manufacture.

Another plate with match marked pieces (*190*) is shown (5.40). Again, it is cast in two pieces, but the casting is finer than that shown in plate 5.39, but not as good as that shown below. This next plate (5.41) shows a fine untouched example of these plates. It consists of two smoothly cast pieces with their backs recessed, and with both pieces match marked *164*.

A post-1870 plate in this third group, which accompanied a cased Tiffany presentation sword to Rear Admiral James Hooker Strong USN (1814-1882)[22]

5.36 Laurel wreath belt plate on leather belt. (Peter Tuite)

5.37 Details of laurel wreath belt plate. (Peter Tuite)

5.38 Laurel wreath belt plate by Joseph Starkey. (Dr. Allen D. Phillips)

5.39 Civil War period laurel wreath belt plate on leather. (Peter Tuite)

5.40 Silver plated laurel wreath belt plate. (John A. Frost)

5.41 Mint laurel wreath belt plate. (Peter Tuite)

dated 1872, is illustrated (5.42). The features of this relatively late unmarked plate cannot be distinguished from the other plates of this style shown above. The two pieces, including the belt loops, are roughly cast, and the cutout is the same as the others shown.

A post-1900 plate on an ensign or lieutenant junior grade (3 stripes) dress leather and blue cloth belt is shown in 5.43. This belt was supplied by Horstmann, and the leather backing is gilt stamped: *HORSTMANN BROS. & CO,/TRADE MARK/ PHILADELPHIA.* This belt marking would date this to about 1900 – very late for a two piece plate. Both the tongue and wreath (5.44) are cast as single pieces, and the wreath has an articulated cutout for the tongue. The castings are relatively rough for such a late plate, as compared to the quality of the castings shown on 5.41.

Another early twentieth century junior officer's light blue dress belt with hash marks denoting it was worn by a warrant officer is also shown (5.45). Warrant Officers were members of our Navy right from its beginning. There were Warrant Officers on the ships of the Continental Navy during the Revolutionary War. When Congress created our Navy in 1794, it listed the Warrant Officers as the Sailing Masters, Purser, Boatswain, Gunner, Carpenter, Sailmaker, and Midshipman. Navy Warrant Officers began wearing blue and gold stripes in 1853 – on their caps. They had stripes of half-inch wide gold lace separated by a quarter-inch wide stripe of blue cloth. In 1888, Chief

Warrant Officers started wearing the sleeve stripe of a single strip of half-inch wide gold lace broken at intervals by sections of blue thread half an inch wide. In 1919, the other Navy Warrant Officers began wearing sleeve stripes of gold lace broken by sections of blue.[23] This type of belt is not shown in the 1869 regulation patterns, nor in the 1883 and 1886 regulations, so it postdates 1886. Thus, it's unusual to have a two piece plate on this belt. A similar junior officer's dress belt with hashed stripes with a one piece plate is shown below.

As illustrated by the above examples of this pattern variant, there is essentially no difference between the design motif on these plates manufactured in the U.S., even though they were manufactured and worn over a period of 50+ years. As also shown,

5.42 Rear Admiral Strong laurel wreath belt plate on dress belt. (Kevin Hoffman)

5.43 Post-1900 laurel wreath belt plate on Ensign/Lieutenant JG dress belt by Horstmann. (Jack Bethune)

5.44 Details of post-1900 laurel wreath belt plate. (Jack Bethune)

5.45 Warrant officer's dress belt with laurel wreath belt plate. (U.S. Naval Academy Museum)

though, the methods of construction and the quality of the castings did vary. Several factors can be used to generally date them. The construction methods on several of the plates (5.33 and 5.39 above) indicate their manufacture during the Civil War, as does the plate on the George Morris belt (5.35). Rear Admiral Strong's belt plate (5.42) is

indicative of the construction methods used in the 1870s, although there's not much difference between this plate and some of the earlier or later ones. Finally, there's the post-1900 Horstmann plate on the junior officer's belt, which indicates what was being made in the twentieth century. Although it's far from clear where this design motif came from, there are enough of these plates extant to show that it was widely worn by naval officers. Just before the Civil War it appears that naval officers were inclined to wear the larger belt plates, where the wreath touched the belt loops, and wore them in the twentieth century. For the three styles of two piece plates described above, the tongue portion design did not change significantly, and its size remained essentially the same as illustrated (5.46).

5.46 Comparisons of belt plate tongues – pattern and two variants. (Peter Tuite)

The rank of admiral did not exist until the Civil War and Congress authorized nine Rear Admirals in July 16, 1862.[24] Two years later Congress authorized the appointment of a Vice Admiral, David Farragut, from among the nine Rear Admirals: Farragut was appointed to Admiral on July 25, 1866, and David Dixon Porter was appointed Vice Admiral. Stephen Rowan was promoted to Vice Admiral in 1870. Congress did not allow

U. S. Navy Belt Plate—1313—Full Size.

5.47 1877 Horstmann catalogue belt plate graphic

5.48 1883 regulation pattern 1852 graphic

5.49 1883 regulation graphic for Admirals belt with plate

the promotion of any of the Rear Admirals to succeed them, so there were no more Admirals or Vice Admirals by promotion until 1915. There was one exception in 1899, when Congress recognized George Dewey's accomplishments during the Spanish American War and the president appointed him Admiral of the Navy, a rank that no one else held again until 1944. Despite this scarcity of the rank of admiral, the Navy Department took great pains to prescribe a series of flag officer belts from 1869 on.

The 1869 uniform regulations[25] prescribed specific dress belts for Admirals and other ranks, and provided:

The full dress sword belt of an Admiral, Vice Admiral and Rear Admiral will be of blue cloth with a small gold cord around the edge, and one strip of and one strip embroidered white-oak leaves, ½ inch wide, running through the centre, as per pattern.

The sling straps shall be of blue cloth with a small gold thread around the edge, as per pattern.

The full dress sword belt of commodores will be of blue cloth with gold embroidery, as per patterns.

The full-dress sword belts of the different grades below Commodore will be of blue webbing with gold cord woven in, as per patterns.

5.50 Pattern 1905 belt plate on leather. (Peter Tuite)

These dress belts are very different from earlier ones, but undress belts are identical to those prescribed in 1864.

The next major change in the pattern 1852 belts and belt plates was the transition to one piece plates, with the design now including three or six cannon balls below a

5.51 Horstmann belt plate. (Peter Tuite)

67

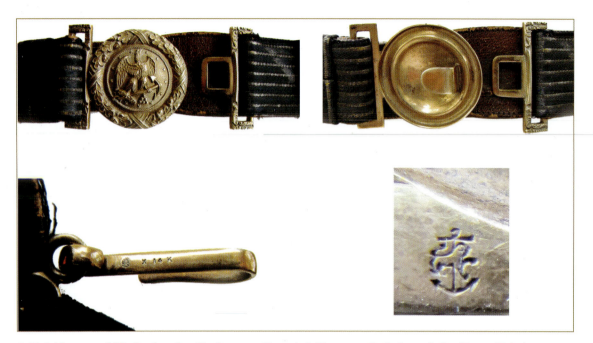

5.52 14 karat gold belt plate by Gorham on Captain's/Commander's dress belt. (Peter Tuite)

slanted anchor. The use of cannon balls below the anchor had been on the Navy's button designs that pre-dated the Civil War. Additionally, one piece plates had been in use since the 1830s, and the two piece plates were being worn after 1900. An 1877 Horstmann catalogue[26] shows a one piece plate (5.47) with the six cannon ball motif, but the 1877 uniform regulations[27] do not contain this graphic, or for that matter any pattern graphics. It isn't until the 1883 uniform regulations that we see a belt plate pattern graphic with the cannon ball motif illustrated in color (5.48).

The 1883 regulations also contained a pattern graphic for an Admiral's belt with plate (5.49), but the plate on this graphic is identical to that presented in the 1869

5.53 Commander Richard Wainwright's dress belt with belt plate. (U.S. Naval Academy Museum)

regulations, although the belt differs. This is an obvious disconnect in the regulations. It appears that the parties preparing the color plates for belts did not check with the parties preparing the color plate for the new belt plate.

A number of examples for one piece plates are presented. The first example (5.50) compares the large wreath two piece pattern plate on leather to a pattern 1905[28] one piece belt plate on leather. The popularity of the larger plates discussed earlier is evident. In addition to the six cannon balls below the slant anchor, the wreath is enlarged to touch the belt loops. On this plate, the eagle sits on a slightly slanted anchor with its head almost straight up through the stars, with six cannon balls below and nine stars above, all within a relatively heavy rope surround. The wreath has the acorn and oak leaf design motif, but is thinner than on the earlier plate shown. The plate casting is relatively thin with a smooth outer periphery and a recess, where the wreath is pronounced. It contains a single clasp for the belt loop attachment soldered to the plate. The belt loops are ornate with flowers at each corner.

The next example (5.51) was supplied by Horstmann, and the back of the plate is stamped with a semi-circular *Horstmann* over *Philada*. Both pieces are match marked *49* on their backs. The eagle is raised relative to the two piece plates and the one above, with its head through the stars, and the array of thirteen stars is continuous, with six stars below the slightly slanted anchor. The eagle

and stars are also surrounded by a heavy rope surround. Like the one above, the casting is thin with a smooth back finish, and the clasp is soldered to it. The belt loops are also ornate with cutout where they almost touch the wreath. This plate is not as detailed as the one in 5.50.

A presentation quality Captain's or Commander's dress belt,[29] with its seven stripes, is shown (5.52). This belt and plate were supplied by Gorham, and all of its furniture is 14 karat gold and so marked. This plate is exquisitely made. The eagle sits on a relatively steeply slanted anchor with six cannon balls and 5 stars below, all within the heavy rope surround on a lined background. The acorn oak leaf wreath is deeply chased and smooth around its periphery. The belt loops are ornate, with cutout where they almost touch the wreath.

Richard Wainwright (USN 1868-1926),[30] then a Commander in the Navy, received a presentation sword made by Tiffany for his actions while in command of the USS *Glouchester* on July 1898 during the Spanish American War.[31] The dress belt, with seven stripes, that accompanied this sword is illustrated (5.53). The design motif on this highly gilded belt plate (5.54) is essentially the same as the Horstmann supplied plate shown in 5.49. The construction details are also essentially the same, indicating that this style one piece plate was worn through the nineteenth century.

The next example is also on a Captain or Commander's seven stripe dress belt (5.55),

but the belt plate is stylized. This plate (5.56) only has three cannon balls below the slightly slanted anchor with three stars below, and the almost upright eagle's head is through the array of stars. The wreath design motif is the laurel wreath with berries, with a single tie at its base, and its periphery is smooth. The belt loops are elaborate and triangular in shape, changing the entire appearance of the plate. The plate pieces are cast with flat backs, and what would be the tongue in a two piece plate is a separate piece and attached to the wreath with two studs. The clasp is soldered to the wreath back. The clasp is stamped *N.S. Meyer/Wash DC*, and the belt plate backing piece is also stamped

5.54 Commander Richard Wainwright belt plate details. (U.S. Naval Academy Museum)

69

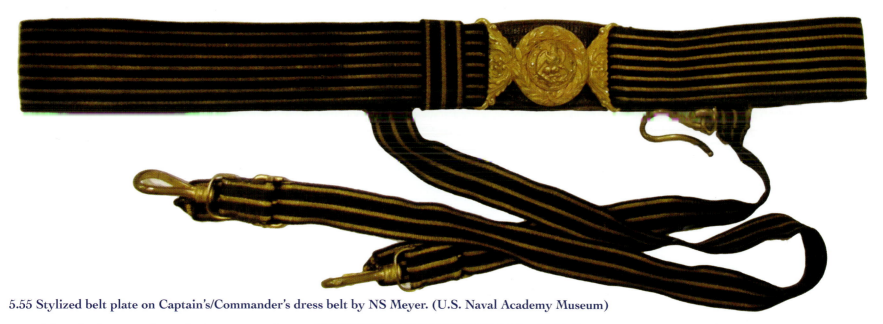

5.55 Stylized belt plate on Captain's/Commander's dress belt by NS Meyer. (U.S. Naval Academy Museum)

in gold with their trademark (see inset plate 5.55). Nathan S. Meyer was in business in New York City from about 1878.[32]

The Navy issued new uniform regulations in 1886[33] and 1897,[34] but the graphic for the pattern belt plate did not change. In its 1905 uniform regulations[35] the pattern graphic did change, and color plates were discontinued (5.57). Unlike the 1883 pattern drawing, this pattern clearly illustrates a one piece belt plate. The design motif has also been changed relative to the 1883 pattern graphic. The eagle is facing up with only its beak through the array of stars, and the slightly slanted anchor has been lowered, with six cannon balls and four stars below it. The background is still lined, and the eagle, anchor, and stars are with the heavy rope surround. The wreath is essentially the same, as are the belt loops.

5.56 Stylized belt plate details. (U.S. Naval Academy Museum)

5.57 1905 regulation pattern graphic

This graphic is repeated in the 1913[36] and 1917[37] regulations.

An example of a Lieutenant's dress belt with five stripes[38] is shown (5.58). This belt was owned by Lieutenant Horace W. Jones (USN 1880-1899).[39.] The design motifs on this plate (5.59) are essentially identical to the 1905 pattern graphic, down to the number of stars below the anchor. It is constructed of

70

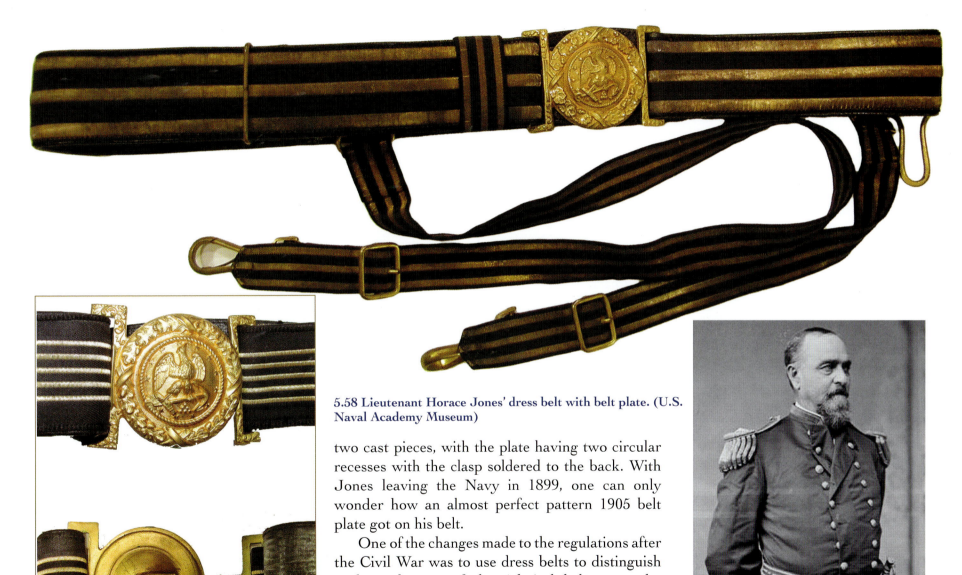

5.58 Lieutenant Horace Jones' dress belt with belt plate. (U.S. Naval Academy Museum)

5.59 Horace Jones belt plate details. (U.S. Naval Academy Museum)

Commodore Robert W Shufeldt c1880 wearing Admiral's Belt. (USN)

two cast pieces, with the plate having two circular recesses with the clasp soldered to the back. With Jones leaving the Navy in 1899, one can only wonder how an almost perfect pattern 1905 belt plate got on his belt.

One of the changes made to the regulations after the Civil War was to use dress belts to distinguish rank, and some of the Admiral belts worn by officers during this period were very attractive. The next example (5.60) illustrates an Admiral's belt made by Horstmann. The belt, made of blue cloth with leather backing, has the three ¼ inch gold

5.60 Admiral's belt with belt plate by Horstmann. (U.S. Naval Academy Museum)

5.61 Details of Admiral's belt plate. (U.S. Naval Academy Museum)

stripes, signifying the belt is to be worn by Rear Admirals and Commodores in the 1883 regulations. The belt plate shown (5.61) is typical and consistent with the 1905 pattern and the belt plate on the Lieutenant's belt above (5.59). The gold embossed Horstmann stamp on the leather indicates that this belt was made in the early 1900s.

Another Admiral belt that accompanied a presentation sword[39] given to Rear Admiral John Woodward Phillip (USN 1861-1899)[40] during the Spanish American War for his actions while in command of the *Texas* off

Rear Admiral William Sampson wearing Admiral's Belt, c1900. (U.S. Naval Academy Museum)

5.62 Rear Admiral John Woodward Phillip's dress belt with plate by Tiffany. (U.S. Naval Academy Museum)

5.63 Details of Tiffany silver belt plate. (U.S. Naval Academy Museum)

Santiago on 3 July 1898 is shown (5.62). The sword was made by Tiffany, as was the fine gilded silver belt plate. The belt has three gold embroidered ½ inch stripes on dark blue velvet cloth with leather backing. The 1883 regulations for Rear Admirals prescribe three ¼ inch wide stripes, so Tiffany took some liberties with this belt with the wider stripes. The plate design motif (5.63) is similar to the 1883 pattern graphic in terms of its depiction of the eagle and steeply slanted anchor, but it only has three cannon balls and four stars below the anchor. Aside from the quality of the circular portion of the plate, it is distinguished by the unique shape of the belt loops and their elaborate design motifs of acorns and oak leaves. The plate is cast and the back is marked Tiffany.

During WWI, Admiral William Benson (USN 1877-1919)[41] was responsible for transporting the Army to France and received a presentation sword[42] from the Daughters of the Confederacy for his efforts. The Admiral belt shown (5.64) accompanied this sword. This belt has the two ½ inch gold stripes with a ¼ inch center stripe as prescribed for Admiral of the Navy in the 1905 regulations. Benson was not Admiral of the Navy, so the supplier took some liberties with the belt. This blue velvet cloth belt with leather backing was made by *Pettibone Bros. Mfg*, as is stamped in green ink on the leather backing. Pettibone was in business in Cincinnatti, Ohio, and doing business from 1894.[42] The belt plate shown (5.65), although highly gilded, is typical of the 1905 pattern, as is its construction.

5.64 Admiral William Benson's dress belt with belt plate by Pettibone. (U.S. Naval Academy Museum)

5.65 Admiral Benson belt plate details. (U.S. Naval Academy Museum)

5.66 Typical undress leather belt with Pattern 1905 belt plate. (Peter Tuite)

Following the Civil War naval officers also wore undress leather belts, and a typical belt plate on leather is shown next (5.66). This belt plate is also typical of the 1905 pattern.

An imported belt plate supplied by Starkey is also shown (5.67). This plate is on an Ensign or Junior Grade Lieutenant's dress belt with three stripes. The plate design is the typical 1905 pattern, but with three cannon balls instead of the patterned six. The plate back is stamped *J. Starkey/23 Conduit St./ London* and is also stamped with the Starkey trademark. The belt plate leather backing piece has similar markings in gold gilt.

5.67 Ensign/Lieutenant JG dress belt with 1905 belt plate by Joseph Starkey. (Peter Tuite)

5.68 Warrant officer's dress belt with 1905 belt plate. (U.S. Naval Academy Museum)

5.69 Pattern 1905 warrant officer's belt plate on dress belt. (U.S. Naval Academy Museum)

5.70 Pattern 1941 belt plate on leather. (Peter Tuite)

A striking black cloth Warrant Officer's belt with gold hash marks is illustrated (5.68). The belt plate (5.69) with three cannon balls below the eagle conforms to the 1905 regulation pattern.

This belt plate design, initiated in 1852, would continue through 1941, when the Navy issued new uniform regulations.[43] These regulations would change the orientation of the eagle from facing its heraldic left to facing its heraldic right. An example of a post-1941 leather belt with plate is shown (5.70). As illustrated, except for the eagle orientation, the other features of the belt plate design are essentially unchanged. This design continues to the present day.

Chapter
6

U.S. MARINE CORPS BELTS AND PLATES

The Continental Congress authorized a corps of Marines, consisting of two battalions of sea soldiers, on November 10, 1775. Following the Revolutionary War the Marines were essentially disbanded like the other services, and it wasn't until an Act of Congress on 11 July 1798 that the present Marine Corps was created. In June 1812 the Corps consisted of 10 officers and 483 men, and by June 1814 it grew to 11 officers and 579 men. On 17 October 1820 Colonel Archibald Henderson became Commandant, and he would serve in this capacity through 7 January 1859. During his almost 30 year tenure he greatly influenced what was worn by officers and enlisted men. The officer corps grew gradually to 19 officers in June 1820 and to 58 officers in 1834, when the Corps became a separate sea service in the

Navy. Table 6.1 shows the rolls for Marine officers from 1840 to 1861.[1,2] Colonel John Harris was appointed commandant to succeed Henderson based on his seniority, and morale suffered under his leadership. When the Civil War broke out, 16 of 31 Captains and 1st Lieutenants went South, decimating the officer ranks commanded by Harris. After the war, Corps strength was reduced from 90 to 78 officers and 1,200 privates. Harris' tenure ended on 12 May 1864.

This chapter addresses the evolution of belts and plates from the early 1800s through the Civil War. The information available on cap and belt plates worn by enlisted Marines and their officers during this early

period is primarily based on Quartermaster correspondence, as there were few explicit regulations until 1839, and the small size of the force significantly reduced the numbers of examples extant.

Marine officers were wearing shoulder belt plates in the early 1800s, as evidenced by several portraits.[3] The first printed order for USMC officers, issued on 14 October 1805,

Table 6.1

USMC OFFICERS					
	1840	1849	1852	1854	1861
COMMANDER/GENERAL STAFF	1	5	5	5	6
LIEUTENANT COLONEL	1	1	1	1	1
MAJOR	4	4	5	5	4
CAPTAIN	13	17	14	14	13
FIRST LIEUTENANT	20	24	20	20	19
SECOND LIEUTENANT	20	24	20	20	20
TOTALS	59	75	65	65	63

c1809 portrait of 1st Lt. Lee Massey with shoulder belt plate. (National Museum of the Marine Corps)

Pre-1812 Lt. William Sharpe Bush with eagle shoulder belt plate. (National Museum of the Marine Corps)

Lt. Addison Garland c1825 wearing a waist belt plate. (National Museum of the Marine Corps)

provided for: *black belts with yellow mounting,* but this order was quickly revised on 16 December 1805 to provide for: *white cross belts with gilt plates.*[4] Another order on 19 May 1810 continued this by providing that officers' side arms should consist of: *yellow-mounted sabers with gilt scabbards, and white cross belts with Gilt plates.*[5] The exact nature of these gilt plates is not specified, but we know that during this period officers were wearing white shoulder belts with an oval plate with eagle in relief. As we see in later years,[6] it was not uncommon for Marine Officers to wear naval plates, so the oval shoulder belt plates shown in chapter two could also have been worn by Marine officers. A pre-

1812 portrait of Marine Lieutenant William Sharpe Bush[7] shows a shoulder belt plate that appears to have a silver oval with eagle at its center and a brass surround. Bush was killed in action during the engagement between the USS *Constitution* and HMS *Guerriere* on 19 August 1812, so his portrait predates the engagement. A c1809 portrait of 1st Lieutenant Lee Massey shows a similar shoulder plate being worn.

As early as 17 October 1798, enlisted men were wearing black belts less than two inches wide[8] and naval buttons with the Armitage motif (*see* plate 2.7), and this continued at least through 5 January 1801.[9] On 5 June 1805, a contract was issued to

6.1 c1807 cap plate die sample "Marines" above and "Fortitudine" below. (American History Museum)

6.2 c1807 cap plate with clipped corners - "Marines" above and "Fortitudine" below. (National Museum of the Marine Corps)

6.3 c1810 officer's belt plate. (Dr. Allen D. Phillips)

Innes and Kinsey for 25 sword belts of the same leather as then in use for cartridge boxes.[10] The color of these belts is not known, but we know that white leather belts were in use a few years later, as Captain Anthony Gale raised the issue of belt color (white versus black) in a March 1808 letter to Navy Commodore John Rodgers.[11] The use of white belts during the War of 1812 is also confirmed in an 1813 letter from Commandant Wharton referring to *buff belts* and belt plates.[12] Thus, enlisted Marines were wearing white bayonet shoulder belts and white waist belts from about 1808, both

with belt plates. Like officers' gilt plates, the exact nature of the enlisted belt plates is not specified in regulations.

The first description of officers' belt plates was in an order on 21 May 1821, which provided that field officers and captains wear white cross belts with gilt plates and an eagle in relief.[13] The Marines had been wearing eagle plates from the early 1800s. George Armitage[14] was making both small (6 cents) and large eagle (25 cents) hat plates and buttons from at least August 1804. Edmund Kinsey,[15] a Philadelphia saddler (1804 to about 1840), was providing enlisted men's sword belts in June 1805. It appears that Kinsey remained a supplier to the Corps, and in February 1811 he would receive an order for 150 caps with eagle plates. In this same time frame Moritz Fürst,[16] a prominent die maker who worked at the Philadelphia Mint, was designing plates for both the Army and the Marines. Robert Dingee,[17] another prominent New York saddler and

accoutrement supplier, was also providing caps, sword belts, cockades, and cartridge boxes primarily to the Army, but also to the Marines. Dingee would remain in business through the Civil War.

The 1821 uniform regulations provided for beaver caps with: *a gilt or gold plate with an eagle on it in front of the cap*.[18] A leather cap with *a brass eagle and plate* was also prescribed for enlisted men.[19] On 29 May 1824 an order for white waist belts was issued,[20] and on 3 May 1825 mention is made of a *white cross belt with a gilt breast plate, scarlet sash made of silk*[21] for enlisted men. In 1825, a *white cross belt with gilt breast plate* and leather caps with *a yellow eagle in front* were also prescribed for officers.[22] The discussion that follows will address known examples of sample dies and cap and belt plates that show Marine Corps motifs, specifically the eagle and anchor.

The earliest recognized uniquely Marine Corps motif consisted of an eagle with upswept head facing its heraldic left on a horizontal anchor resting on a cannon surrounded by stands of arms with flags, with a banner reading *Fortitudine* (with courage) above in script and the word *Marines* in capital letters below. An example of a die sample is illustrated (6.1). Two of these die samples are presently residing in museums: one at the Smithsonian and one at the U.S. Marine Corps Museum. One of these die samples was first discussed in a 1963 Smithsonian *Bulletin*[23] that indicated that the 1804 Marine Corps regulations specified a *Brass Eagle and Plate*, and that the 1807 regulations called for *Octagon Plates*. The *Bulletin* also indicates that a dug sample of a plate with this exact motif, somewhat enlarged but with clipped corners, was excavated at a known naval shore station in 1959. These findings would indicate that this uniquely Marine motif, in the form of a cap plate, pre-dated the War of 1812. An illustration of this motif on an octagonal cap

plate is also shown (6.2). Another example of this motif can be seen on a belt plate (6.3), the only known example of this motif as a belt plate. The writing above and below the eagle amid arms is eliminated, and the edges are rolled to effect smooth edges. Belt attachments in the form of two studs and a clasp have been soldered to the plate rear. The plate has also been made thicker to function with a belt, as opposed to being attached to a cap. The designer of this unique motif has not yet been identified. However, the design of the eagle's head and beak and its orientation is very similar to another belt plate attributed to George Armitage,[24] so attributing this plate design to George Armitage would not be unreasonable.

The infantry were wearing oval shoulder belt plates, both plain and with designs, since about 1812, and it has been learned from Quartermaster correspondence that eagle and anchor plates were provided to

6.5 Excavated 1804-1815 hat plate or cockade inscribed "Marines." (Troiani Collection)

Marines as early as the War of 1812.[25] A distinctly Marine shoulder belt plate is next illustrated (6.4). The design motif is an

6.4 c1815 officer's shoulder belt plate inscribed "Marines." (Dr. Allen D. Phillips)

6.6 1804-1815 hat plate or cockade inscribed "Marines." (Dr. Allen D. Phillips)

80

6.7 c1826 shoulder belt plate die sample. (American History Museum)

intaglio engraved primitive eagle with slightly upswept wings facing its heraldic right while standing on a horizontal fouled anchor. There is a banner that reads *MARINES* above and a leaf and flower garland below. Its construction is similar to other oval plates of this era – thin rolled brass that is die-struck to define the motif and raised border over a thin iron backing. A three pronged continuous wire belt hook is soldered to the plate back. The nature of the engraving indicates that this plate was manufactured c1815 and was probably worn by a Marine officer.[26] The reverse is also lightly stamped *T. SMITH*. The mark *T SMITH N-YORK* has also appeared on the back of a white metal 2 1/2 inch diameter eagle plate on a pattern 1828 bayonet shoulder belt.[27]

Thaddeus Smith was a metal worker in New York City from 1808-1835, and he subcontracted plates to Robert Dingee, who supplied leather goods and accoutrements to the Army and Marine Corps.

Two examples of an early (1804-1815) Marine plate are extant and both are illustrated (6.5 and 6.6). While the first example (6.5) was excavated and is missing a small section, the level of detail is comparable to the non-excavated example. This design oval plate has an eagle with upswept wings facing its heraldic left on a slanted fouled anchor with *MARINES* above. It is constructed of thin rolled brass plate that is die-struck to define the motif and raised border with a solder backing. This plate does not have any belt or

cap plate attachment pieces on its back – just four sets of two small holes each around its periphery. It is not a belt plate, but the sets of double sew holes indicate it was a cap plate or cockade.

The 1825 order for enlisted men provided for white waist and shoulder belts, with the oval shoulder belt plate including an eagle in relief. However, in an 1828 Order Commandant Henderson required that the oval brass shoulder belt plate be plain.[28] An example of this plain oval plate is in the Smithsonian collection, and it is illustrated in other works.[29] This plain oval brass plate would be worn by Marine Corps officers until the early 1870s.

6.8 c1826 shoulder belt plate sample. (Peter Tuite)

81

Another plate motif attributable to the Marines consists of an eagle facing its heraldic left with upswept wings perched on a slanted anchor and stand of colors with shield and varied stand of arms below (6.7). There is no inscription on the plate. Like the one above (see 6.1), this motif was first discussed in the Smithsonian *Bulletin*.[30] The example discussed was a die sample (6.7). As shown, the motif is displayed within an oval within a rectangular plate with small holes at its corners. Based on the information then available, the plate could not be dated later than 1825. More research has been done, and there is evidence that this plate motif was designed by Moritz Fürst. Earlier he had made the dies for the 1812-1815 series of cap plates, and in early 1826 he was also

6.9 c1826 shoulder belt plate sample tag. (Peter Tuite)

6.10 c1826 shoulder belt plate. (Dr. Allen D. Phillips)

invited to make several specimens of dies for belts and caps for trial.[31] The design was never formally adopted by the Army, but some showed up on the commercial market. One of Fürst's letters dated 29 March 1826 indicates he was making two dies for breast plates: one for Marines and one for the Army.[32] These plates were intended to be worn with the pattern 1828 bayonet shoulder belts, but both were rejected. There is also a sample plate with the same design motif (6.8). This is a die struck rolled brass plate with two hook attachments soldered to its back. No lead has been added to strengthen the plate. This plate was accompanied by a tag that reads: *Sample submitted by B depot Quartermaster US Marine Corps Philadelphia* (6.9). This was probably the shoulder

6.11 c1820 shako bell cap with cap plate. (Private Collector)

6.12 1852 USN regulation graphic for USMC lieutenant's hat plate

6.13 1852 USN regulation graphic for USMC button

belt plate sample that Fürst submitted for consideration by the Marines in 1826.

The Fürst design motif on the above shoulder belt plate sample also presents itself on two known examples of shoulder belt plates. This shoulder belt plate (6.10) is identical to the sample plate except for its back. It is also a die struck rolled brass plate with a continuous wire belt hook soldered to the back. Unlike the sample, lead has been added to the back to strengthen the plate, and it shows some wear. Despite these extant examples, Fürst never received a contract to supply either belt or cap plates to the Marine Corps.

The eagle and anchor motif also appeared on early USMC cap plates. Before the eagle and anchor was adopted, officers were wearing a simple eagle on their bell shako

6.14 c1846 eagle and anchor hat plate die sample. (American History Museum)

6.15 Two c1846 eagle and anchor hat plates. (John A. Gunderson and Pat Regis)

caps with the eagle facing its heraldic right. The only known example of this shako cap with eagle plate is illustrated (6.11). The first cap plate defined with the eagle on slanted anchor was illustrated in the Navy's 1852 uniform regulations[33] for cap plates (6.12) and buttons (6.13). The design for the cap plate shows the eagle on slanted anchor on a shield and surrounded by laurel sprigs on each side (6.12). It appears, though, that the eagle on slanted anchor shown was usually worn without the 1852 pattern plate embellishments of laurel sprigs.[34] It may well be that the embellished plate design in the 1852 regulations pre-dates those shown here. Several examples of the eagle on slanted

anchor cap plate, without embellishment, are extant and are illustrated. The first (6.14) has no wear and appears to be a die sample. The other two shown together (6.15) have slightly different configurations, indicating there was more than one manufacturer of these devices. It is believed that these cap devices were worn as early as 1846. The 1859 uniform regulations replaced the eagle on anchor with a bugle with an *M* in the center, and this motif was in use through late 1868. An order replaced the bugle motif on caps with the eagle, globe, and anchor (EGA) device that is still in use today.[35] An example of the eagle, globe, and anchor hat device is shown (6.16).

6.16 Eagle, anchor, and globe hat plate. (Pat Regis)

6.17 c1850 enlisted French clasp belt plate by Horstmann. (Dr. Allen D. Phillips)

essentially the same. Another example of this plate type can be seen in an earlier work.[37]

These belt plates would be worn by enlisted Marines until the early 1870s.

The next example of a belt and plate is believed to have been worn by Levi Twiggs during his early career. The white cloth belt and round brass plate with eagle in relief is shown (6.18).

Twiggs was married to the granddaughter of Stephen Decatur, and the belt was passed down through the Decatur family as being

The 1831 uniform regulations prescribed white belts with brass belt plates for enlisted men. These requirements remained in effect through at least 1859, since enlisted men's belts and plates are not mentioned in the 1839 uniform regulations. The 1859 uniform regulations prescribed: *white waist belts of the French pattern with the French clasp and knapsack sliding slings*.[36] It is not clear that these requirements affected what types of belts and plates enlisted men were wearing from 1831. The examples extant for these enlisted men's waist belt plates are very similar, and an example of one made by Horstmann is shown (6.17). It is a thick, slightly convex brass plate with two brass studs fitted with oval washers and a tongue all soldered to the plate back. The tongue is stamped *Horstmann/Phila*. Horstmann had a contract for these belt plates for one year (1852-1853). Most plates were provided by William Pinchin of Philadelphia, who had a contract with the Marine Corps to provide these belt plates from the 1830s through 1856. Pinchin had

6.18 Cloth white belt with militia belt plate worn by USMC Major Levi Twiggs. (Jack Bethune)

acquired the business from George Armitage in about 1825, and was a major supplier to both the Army and Marine Corps. Other extant plates by different manufacturers have slightly different stud and tongue configurations, but the faces of the plates are

his. He was born in Georgia on 21 May 1793, and was commissioned a 2nd Lieutenant in the Marine Corps in 1813. In 1815, he was promoted to First Lieutenant, and to Captain in 1830. In 1836, he fought the Creeks and

6.19 USMC Major Levi Twiggs' belt plate details. (Jack Bethune)

Seminoles during the Florida-Georgia Indian Wars. In 1840, after ten years as a Captain, he was promoted to Major, and was ordered to combat duty in the Mexican War in 1847. Major Twiggs commanded a storming party on Chapultepec Castle, and while leading this detachment in the assault on the castle he was killed by enemy fire.

While the belt is white cotton with brass chain slings, indicating possible use by a USMC officer, the round belt plate with eagle is consistent with plates worn by militia officers in the 1830s.[38] The two-piece plate details are also illustrated (6.19), with each piece stamped 5.

On 1 July 1839, a set of uniform regulations was issued addressing uniforms for both enlisted men and officers. For officers, the wearing of the Mameluke-hilted sword and a white leather sword belt with sliding frog[39] from 1834 was repeated as follows:

Sword belt – White leather, two inches wide, with sliding frog, to be worn around the waist, over the coat and clasped in front; clasp, according to the a pattern to be furnished by the Quartermasters Department.

These regulations were supplemented with an Order issued on 23 January 1840 that prescribed officers' caps, undress sword belts in black leather with matching slings, and the standard M1839 belt plate as follows:

4. All Officers of the corps, when in uniform and not in full dress, will wear the following described cap, belt and plate, from and after the fourth of July, 1840.

5. Cap, blue cloth, with a black patent leather visor, the segment of a circle; a twilled silk band to surround the body of the cap, with silver German text letters, U.S.M., in a gold wreath in front three-fourths of an inch wide, with a small marine button on each side of the cap; the upper part of the crown to be extended by a whalebone hoop. [Note that this cap design was only in effect for one year. It was replaced by an anchor within a wreath.]

6. Belt. The undress belt to be of black patent leather; the sword to be suspended by black patent leather; swivels of brass to receive the sword.

7. Plate for the belts to be of plain brass of oblong form, three inches in length and two inches wide, with a gold wreath of raised work within it; German text letters "USM" of silver (likewise raised work) of the same pattern and dimensions as the work on the fatigue cap.

6.20 1852 USN regulation graphic for USM 1839 belt plate

There are no provisions in either Order addressing enlisted men's caps, belts, or belt plates. Thus, the earlier provisions would govern.

As of 4 July 1840, officers would be obliged to wear either a white leather sword belt with sliding frog or a black patent leather (undress) belt with slings, both of which bore the same 1839 belt plate bearing the letters *USM*. The pattern for this belt plate would be published later in the Navy's 1852 regulations,[40] the first time USMC uniform regulations were accompanied by pattern drawings, which was something the Navy initiated in 1830.

In 1840 there were 59 USMC officers in service, so few examples of the *USM* belt plate are extant. The pattern drawing published in the 1852 Navy uniform regulations is shown (6.20). The information presented in an earlier work by Bill Gavin[41] on belt plates would indicate that there were at least two different manufacturers of these plates, since he found two slightly different belt

6.21 Graphic comparing 1839 belts plate. (Bill Gavin)

plate configurations. The illustration in the previous work comparing the two different plate configurations is reproduced here (6.21). Note that the upper plate has some space between the wreath and the sides of the plate and conforms to the pattern drawing (see 6.20), while the lower plate drawing shows the wreath very close to the plate sides. Gavin also noted a slight difference in overall dimensions: 3 1/4 x 2 1/8 inches for the upper plate and 2 7/8 x 2 inches for the lower one. Construction methods also differed, with the upper plate having the wreath and letters attached by wires and the lower plate having the wreath and letters soldered to the brass plate. Neither of the plates in Gavin's comparison conforms exactly to the pattern, since they both have wreaths composed of oak leaves and acorns on the left and laurel leaves on the right, as opposed to a wreath entirely of laurel leaves.

6.22 Officer's white glazed leather belt with 1839 USM belt plate. (John A. Gunderson)

6.23 Pattern 1839 USM plate details. (John A. Gunderson)

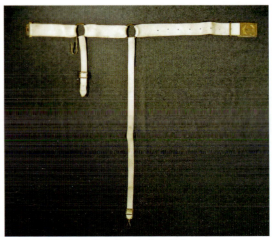

6.24 Buff white leather belt of Commandant Harris with 1839 USM plate.
(National Museum of the Marine Corps)

Three different examples of this belt plate on leather are described. The first example is on a belt (6.22) that appears to have originally been white patent leather (now tan). The belt is one continuous piece, and includes sword belt slings of the same material. As shown, the white patent leather has been blackened, but most of the black has been removed with wear and tear. The plate is also illustrated (6.23). The left side of the wreath has the pattern oak leaf and acorn motif, while the right side has the laurel leaf motif. Both the wreath and the letters are silver, as opposed to the gold wreath and silver letters defined in the Order.

The 1840 Order supplemented the white sword belt with the sliding frog mentioned in the 1839 regulations by adding a black undress belt with slings, which means the original blackened belt followed 1840 regulations. General plate design and construction are similar to that prescribed for Army general and staff officers in its 1832 uniform regulations, and also adopted by the Texas

Navy (*see* plate 2.30), which was made about 1836.

The second example is on a buff white leather belt belonging to Colonel John Harris, Commandant during the Civil War. As shown (6.24), this belt is of much lighter construction and is connected by brass rings to attach the sword belt slings. This belt style is of earlier construction than the one above. The belt plate (6.25) also differs from the one above. The proportions between the wreath and the plate are slightly different: the wreath design differs, the letters differ, and both the wreath and the letters are brass, as opposed to the silver in the first plate. Both these belt plates are the variants referred to by Gavin.

A third example that differs from both of the above plates is shown. This belt is black leather, and is of segmented construction connected with brass rings (6.26). The belt plate (6.27) is as per the pattern drawing

6.25 Detail of Commandant Harris 1839 USM plate.
(National Museum of the Marine Corps)

6.26 Officer's black segmented leather belt with 1839 USM plate. (John A. Frost)

6.27 Detail of 1839 USM plate. (John A. Frost)

(*see* plate 6.20 above), with space between the wreath and belt plate sides and a wreath composed entirely of laurel leaves. Like the first example, the wreath and letters are silver. The three different belt plates are illustrated together for comparison purposes (6.28).

Although these plates are not marked, there is evidence that Ames was the manufacturer of at least one of these plates. Other research has determined three of these pattern 1840 belt plates were ordered from Ames in 1840.[42] An examination of the plate backs indicates that the Harris plate was made by Ames. Like the Texas Navy belt plate by Ames, the plate back includes a

V-cut tongue so the keeper lays flush with the back of the buckle.

The Marine Corps section in the Navy's 1852 uniform regulations provided:

Sword-Belt

White leather, two inches wide, with sliding frog, to be worn round the waist, over the coat, and clasped in front: clasp, according to a pattern to be furnished by the Quartermaster's Department.

The pattern 1839 belt plate would thus remain in use until 1859, when Marine uniform regulations would again be issued in October. In these regulations,[43] the Marines adopted the eagle-on-wreath belt

Lt. Cash with 1839 Belt Plate and c1846 Cap Plate. (Peter Buxtun)

89

6.28 Comparison of 1839 USM belt plates.

plate worn by Army officers and NCOs since 1851. These 1859 Marine regulations provided:

Sword Belt
For all Officers. – A waist belt not less than one and one half inches, nor more than two inches wide, to be worn over the sash; the sword to be suspended from it by slings of the same material as the belt, attached to the belt, upon which the sword may be hung (See Plate Fig. 12)

For the Commandant – Of Russia leather, with three stripes of gold embroidery; the slings embroidered on both sides; or the same belt as to be immediately prescribed for all other officers.

For all other Officers – Of glazed white leather

Sword Belt Plate
For all Officers. – Gilt rectangular, two inches wide, with a raised bright rim, a wreath of laurel encircling the Arms of the United States; eagle, shield, edge of cloud, and rays, bright (See Plate Fig. 13)

Belts
All enlisted men shall wear white waist belts of the French pattern, with the French clasp and knapsack sliding slings…

(For Pattern of Belt, complete, see pattern in the Quartermaster's Office, Head Quarters)

The belt plate illustrations in both the 1851 Army and 1859 Marine Corps uniform regulations are identical, and Fig. 13 in the

Officers' Sword Belt Plate.

6.29 1859 USMC regulation graphic for Pattern 1859 USMC officer's belt plate.

Marine Corps regulations is shown (6.29). This pattern is a familiar one, with the eagle facing its heraldic left with the olive branch placed in the right talon, indicating peaceful intentions, as opposed to the three arrows indicating signs of belligerency in the left talon. Most of the plates seen have the eagle's head turned to the heraldic right, the side of honor. In an earlier study,[44] about 50 examples of the Army's plate for all officers were examined, and only one example had the eagle's head to the heraldic left as per the pattern drawing. The Army apparently changed its pattern graphic for the belt plate prior to 1864,[45] but the Marine Corps retained the pattern graphic with the eagle facing its heraldic left at least until 1912.[46]

An example of this belt plate on leather is shown (6.30). Details of the plate are also shown (6.31). Note that the eagle is facing its heraldic right, contrary to the pattern. Also note that the edge of cloud mentioned in the regulations is missing. The Army plate study cited above that found only one plate with the eagle facing its heraldic left also found that this was the only plate of the 50 that had the edge of cloud motif.

The uniform regulations for Marine Corps belts and plates have changed little from the requirements cited above to the present day. Relevant excerpts for the Corps regulations on belts and plates through 1900 are presented in Appendix B.

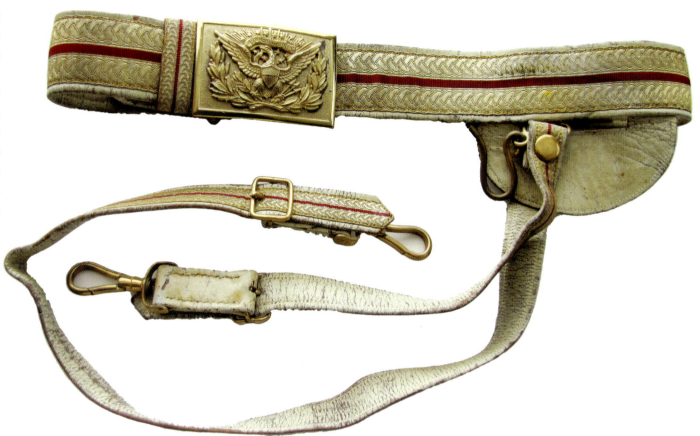

6.30 Pattern 1859 USMC Officer's belt with plate. (Jack Bethune)

6.31 Details of Pattern 1859 belt plate. (Jack Bethune)

Chapter
7

CONFEDERATE STATES NAVY BELTS AND PLATES

The Confederate States Navy (CSN) was formed on February 20, 1861, by *An act for the reorganization of the Navy*,[1] as passed by the Senate and House of Representatives of the Confederate States. This Act prescribed the make up of the Navy by defining ranks from admiral (3) to carpenters (10) for a total complement of 610 officers and rates. The officer ranks would be the same as those in the Confederate Army. This Act also authorized the issuance of letters of Marque for privateers. It was amended on May 9th to provide for the purchase of six steam propeller ships from England, as well as arms and stores to be used by the Navy.

Between the beginning of the Civil War and the spring of 1862, about 370 officers and midshipmen resigned from the United

MEDIUM · **LARGE** · **SMALL**

7.1 CSN Regulation button graphic.

States Navy[2] to serve in the Confederacy. In order to expand the Navy Department to provide positions for all the new officers and recruits, the Confederate Congress passed the *Amendatory Act of April 21, 1862*,[3] which increased the Confederate Navy ranks. By war's end the ranks of the Confederate Navy numbered about 600 officers and about 4000 enlisted men.[4]

The uniform regulations for the Confederate States Navy[5] were issued on 1861. These regulations did not prescribe belt plates, but they did prescribe three buttons:

Buttons shall be of three sizes: large medium and small, and all of the same device, as per pattern.

The pattern button design graphic from the regulations is shown (7.1). Like the U.S. Navy from 1830 on, the CSN would initially use belt plates with the same motif as their pattern uniform buttons. An example of one of these pattern buttons is also illustrated (7.2). This button is back marked *E.M. Lewis & Co., Richmond, Va.*

Very little is known about CSN belts and plates, but we do know that when regulation dolphin head swords were supplied from England they were marked either Courtney & Tennant or Firmin & Sons, and they were accompanied by a leather belt with belt plate. Robert Mole & Sons of Birmingham, England, manufactured weapons for the Confederacy that were imported through Courtney & Tennent of Charleston, South Carolina. Separately, Commander James D. Bulloch, CSN, was sent to England to find military suppliers, and one of his main contacts was Firmin & Sons, a military outfitter. Mole stamped its manufactured

7.2 CSN pattern sailing ship button. (Dr. Allen D. Phillips)

swords and cutlasses with *Mole*, but none of the belt plates described here are so stamped, so the only real basis for attribution is to a supplier, i.e., Courtney & Tennent or Firmin.

One of the rarest CSN belt plates with the regulation pattern sailing ship motif is shown (7.3). This is a false two piece plate that shows a ship under sail surrounded by 13 stars above and below, with the inscription *CSN* below the ship in what would normally be the tongue. The ship is surrounded by a cotton plant wreath that extends beyond the belt loops. Both the wreath and the attachment are cast. It is likely that this plate was made by Firmin & Sons of London.

Another sailing ship based belt plate is shown (7.4). It is likely that this plate was produced domestically. It is of the two piece design, and its construction is similar to that of the U.S. Navy's early pattern 1852 belt plates described in chapter five. Its design

7.3 CSN pattern sailing ship belt plate. (Dr. Allen D. Phillips)

7.4 Variant CSN sailing ship belt plate. (Dr. Allen D. Phillips)

that one of these plates was on a belt with a Firmin dolphin head CSN regulation sword. These belt plates have been widely copied but the two correct specimens on display in museums have been the only ones extant for the last 50 years. One of the known belt plates on brown leather is on display at the Confederate Historical Society, and is shown (7.5). The details for the other known belt plate of this type at the Museum of the Confederacy are also shown (7.6).

In 2012, a third example of these belts with belt plate was discovered. This discovery clearly indicates that these belt plates with brown belt accompanied imported British Beaumont-Adams revolvers known to have been worn by Confederate naval officers. The recently discovered belt, belt plate,

motif is very different than the pattern plate above. The tongue includes a sailing ship with 13 stars above the waves with no inscription. The wreath pattern is comprised of laurel leaves and berries with the inscription *CSN* above the tongue. This wreath is identical to that used on U.S. Navy belt plates as early as 1841 (*see* plate 4.3) and again during the Civil War (*see* plate 5.33). The wreath does not extend to the belt loops as it does on the cited USN belt plates with the same wreaths. The tongue consists of two pieces, with the center medallion attached to the belt loop, and the cutout in the wreath is rectangular with rounded ends. All three pieces of this plate are cast, but the details are not as fine as those on the ship plate shown above. There are three known CSN swords that were manufactured by Boyle and Gamble, and it is possible that this belt plate accompanied one of these swords and pre-dated the imports. Recently, a belt plate of the same design, accompanied by a partial militia scabbard, was excavated.[6]

There is another type of CSN belt plate that is as rare as the pattern ship plate above. These are the two piece plates with the simple motif of a large *CN* on the tongue, surrounded by an unadorned wreath. They have always been assumed to accompany CSN swords or possibly cutlasses. In fact, an earlier author[7] indicates

7.5 CN belt plate on leather. (Virginia Historical Society, Richmond Virginia)

7.6 Details of CN belt plate. (The Museum of the Confederacy, Richmond Virginia, Photo by Alan Thompson)

leather holster, and Adams revolver are shown (7.7). Details of the belt plate are also illustrated (7.8).

The design of these plates is similar to that for the 1839 enlisted Army artillery plates.[7] As shown, the wreath has a rectangular fitted cutout for the tongue and the tongue and wreath are simple castings with the tongue extension brazed or soldered to the tongue. It is notable that none of these belt plates are gilded.

While the regulation pattern for the CSN is the ships plate shown above, the unofficial CSN pattern is the crossed cannon/fouled anchor surrounded by cotton and tobacco plant wreath. These plates are the most prevalent and were all imported. Like the U.S. Navy, CSN belt plates closely followed the design of buttons that were in use. Most of the CSN buttons that incorporate the crossed cannon/fouled anchor design have CSN on them, unlike the belt plates that only have CN. Only Courtney & Tennent supplied buttons have the same motif as this most common CSN belt plate: one button of gilded brass and one button of hard rubber. Examples of both of these buttons with the crossed cannon/anchor and CN below are shown (*see* 7.9 and 7.10)

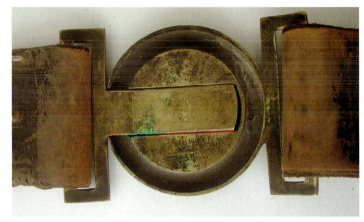

7.8 Details of belt plate accompanying Beaumont-Adams revolver and hostler. (Dr. Allen D. Phillips)

Three examples of these *de facto* pattern belt plates on leather are illustrated in this chapter. The first belt shown (7.11) does not include hangers, and the plate is slightly wider than the belt. The details of the belt plate are also shown (7.12). For this example, the tongue motif is the crossed cannon/fouled anchor on a stippled background with *CN* below. Both the tongue and wreath are match marked *8*. The wreath has the classic CSN cotton plant motif on the right and tobacco plant motif on the left, and just touches the belt loops. The tongue consists of two pieces, with the die stamped center medallion attached to the belt loop extension. The cutout in the wreath is rectangular with rounded ends.

7.7 Belt and belt plate with Beaumont-Adams revolver holster. (Dr. Allen D. Phillips)

7.9 CSN button with CN motif. (Dr. Allen D. Phillips)

7.10 CSN hard rubber button with CN motif. (Harry Ridgeway, Relicman)

7.11 CSN belt plate on leather. (John A. Gunderson)

7.12 CSN Belt Plate Details. (John A. Gunderson)

The next plate on leather (7.13) was worn by William Pickney Mason, a 2nd Lieutenant.[9] Unlike the belt above, this example has a braided leather sword hanger, and the leather plate backing is enlarged to encompass the belt plate wreath. As shown on the plate details (7.14), the tongue motif is the same as that shown above, with the tongue and wreath match marked with an upside down *40*.

Mason was born in Virginia, and resigned from the USN as acting midshipman on 19 April 1861. He was appointed from Virginia as acting midshipman on 11 June 1861 and appointed past midshipman on 3 October 1862. He achieved the rank of Lieutenant on 6 June

7.13 Lt. William Pinckney Mason CSN Belt Plate on Leather. (The Museum of the Confederacy, Richmond Virginia, Photo by Alan Thompson)

Confederate Navy Officers in Virginia Navy Uniforms, one with Firmin Sword and Belt. (Peter Tuite)

7.14 Lt. William Pinckney Mason CSN Belt Plate Details. (The Museum of the Confederacy, Richmond, Virginia, Photo by Alan Thompson)

1864. He saw considerable sea service during the war. He served on CSRS *United States* in 1861, the James River Squadron 1861-1862, Drewry's Bluff in 1862, and CSS *Jamestown* in 1862. He went abroad on special services in 1863-1864 and later served on CSS steamers *Beaufort* and *Virginia*, James River Squadron, 1863-1864.

The third example on leather (7.15) was worn by Acting Master's Mate Lodge Colton.[10] Like the one above, this belt includes the braided leather sword hanger, but the plate leather backing differs. Colton was from Maryland, and joined the Confederate Navy in Baltimore. He served on the CSN cruiser *Shenandoah* until the end of the war.

7.15 Acting master lodge Colton CSN belt plate on leather. (The Museum of the Confederacy, Richmond, Virginia, Photo by Alan Thompson)

7.16 Acting master lodge Colton CSN belt plate details. (The Museum of the Confederacy, Richmond, Virginia, Photo by Alan Thompson)

99

7.17 Variant CSN belt plate. (Dr. Allen D. Phillips)

Another plate of this design with a slightly different wreath motif is also illustrated (7.17). Again, we see the tongue with the crossed cannon/anchor motif with *CN* below on a stippled background. The wreath, with a cotton and tobacco plant motif that differs from those previously shown, just touches the belt loops. The plate is japanned, and the tongue consists of two pieces with the center medallion attached to the belt loop. The cutout in the wreath is rectangular with rounded ends. The tongue medallion is stamped. This variant would indicate that there were at least two makers of these belt plates.

Another rare CSN plate on leather (7.18) was worn by Captain Robert Baker Pegram.[11] This belt was accompanied by a

After the war he settled in Philadelphia and married in 1882. He was last known to be alive in Philadelphia in 1910 at age 73. It is notable that this belt was accompanied by a regulation dolphin head sword supplied by Courtney and Tennant. The Colton plate details (7.16) are identical to those for the other two examples, except the pieces are match marked with an upside down *19* on the wreath and a sideways *19* on the tongue.

The belt plates on all three leather belts above are essentially identical, except for the match marks, which from the Colton provenance would indicate they were supplied by Courtney and Tennent, with the leather belts obtained from different makers.

7.18 Captain Robert Baker Pegram's one piece CSN belt plate on leather. (Brooks Holder)

7.19 Captain Robert Pegram's one piece CSN belt plate details. (Brooks Holder)

regulation CSN officer's sword made by Firmin & Sons, so it can be assumed that this false two piece plate was supplied by Firmin. Unlike the belts shown above, this leather belt is relatively narrow and has the flat leather strap sword hanger like the USN belts of the period.

Pegram was born in Virginia on 10 December 1811, and entered the United States Navy as a midshipman 2 February 1829. He served in the Mediterranean, Japan, and East India Squadrons, and in the famous Wilkes Expedition. His most celebrated service was the capture of a piratical flotilla in the Sea of China. He took sixteen Junks with one hundred cannons, inflicting a loss of one hundred men. He received recognition from the British Commander in the expedition, and her Majesty, Queen Victoria.

Pegram resigned from the USN as Lieutenant on 17 April 1861, and was appointed Captain in the Provisional Navy. He was initially placed in command of the Norfolk Navy Yard, where he disabled the steamer *Harriet Lane* with his batteries at Pigs Point. He then commanded the steamer *Nashville* and captured the *Harvey Burch* in the English Channel. He also superintended the armament of the iron-clad *Richmond*. Funds were raised to purchase what was termed the volunteer navy of the State. He went to England for that purpose and had a vessel ready when Appomattox occurred. His sword of honor, bestowed upon him by a grateful State of Virginia, is now in the Confederate Museum in Richmond. Captain Pegram remained in Norfolk until his death on 24 October 1894.

The Pegram plate (7.19) is a false two piece design with the classic motifs, but without the CN in the tongue section. The wreath slightly overlaps the belt loops, is narrower than the above plates, and the cotton and tobacco plant motif differs from all of the others. Both the plate section and the loop attachment are cast with the fastener attached to the plate section.

The above material discusses all of the known belt plate designs worn by Confederate naval officers during the Civil War, and all but one of these designs were imported from England.

Appendix A:
Excerpts from U.S. Navy
Belt Plate Regulations 1830-1941

Introduction

This Appendix contains excerpts from the United States Navy's Uniform Regulations as they relate to officers belts and plates from 1830 through 1941.

Rules of the Navy Department, Regulating the Civil Administration of the Navy of the United States, 1832

Belts.
Blue webbing for undress; white webbing for dress as per pattern.

Regulations for the Uniforms and Dress of the Navy of the United States, 1841

Swords and belts
… the belt must be made with a frog Belts for undress to be of black leather: for full dress, the belts to be of white webbing, both to be one and a half inch wide; the mountings must be yellow gilt. The swords and mountings, and the mountings of the belt, to be according to pattern.

Regulations for the Uniforms & Dress of the Navy and Marine Corps of the United States 1852

Sword-Belt

For All officers- shall be of plain black glazed leather, not less than one inch and a half nor more than two inches wide, with slings of the same not less than one half nor more than three quarters inch wide and a hook for the forward ring to suspend the sword. Belt plate of yellow gilt in front, two inches in diameter, as per pattern

1869 Pattern graphic

1877 Horstmann catalog

Navy Department, Uniform for Officers of the United States Navy as prescribed in General Order of The Secretary of the Navy, July 31, 1862 (with appendix) (p5)

Sword, Sword Knot and Belt
For All officers-Same as now prescribed for Commissioned Officers

Navy Department, Uniform for Officers of the United States Navy as Prescribed in Regulations for the Uniform of the U.S Navy, Jan. 28, 1864 (p9)

Sword-Belt
265. For All officers- shall be of plain black glazed leather, not less than one inch and a half nor more than two inches wide, with slings of the same not less than one half nor more than three quarters inch wide and a hook for the forward ring to suspend the sword. Belt plate of yellow gilt in front, two inches in diameter, as per pattern

Navy Department, Regulations for the Uniform of the United States Navy, December 1, 1866 (p12) same as 1864 - plate 28 shows the belt for all officers:

Sword-Belt

For all officers shall be of plain black glazed leather, not less than one inch and a half nor more than two inches wide, with slings of the same not less than one-half inch wide nor more than three-quarters of an inch wide, and a hook in the forward ring to suspend the sword. Belt-plate of yellow gilt in front, two inches in diameter, as per pattern. The belt to be worn over the coat.

Uniform for the United States Navy, prepared under the direction of the Secretary of the Navy, Washington, 1869 (p12)

SWORDS, ETC.
SWORD AND SCABBARD

The full dress sword belt of an Admiral, Vice Admiral and Rear Admiral will be of blue cloth with a small gold cord around the edge, and one strip of and one strip embroidered white-oak leaves, ½ inch wide, running through the centre, as per pattern.
The sling straps shall be of blue cloth with a small gold thread around the edge, as per pattern.
The full dress sword belt of commodores will be of blue cloth with gold embroidery, as per patterns.
The full-dress sword belts of the different grades below Commodore will be of blue webbing with gold cord woven in, as per patterns.

UNDRESS SWORD BELT.

For all officers shall be of plain black glazed leather, not less than one inch and a half nor more than two inches wide, with slings of the same not less than one-half inch wide nor more than three-quarters of an inch wide, and a hook in the forward ring to suspend the sword. Belt-plate of yellow gilt in front, two inches in diameter. The belt to be worn over the coat.

Navy Department, Regulations for the Government of the Navy of the United States 1876, Appendix 3, 1877 (p13)

Sword and Sword Belts

The dress sword belt of the Admiral and Vice-Admiral will be of navy blue cloth with a small gold cloth around the edge, and one strip of gold-embroidered white oak leaves, one half inch wide, running through the center, as per pattern.

The sling straps to be of blue cloth with a small gold thread around the edge. The full dress sword belts for the grades below the rank of Vice-Admiral will be of blue webbing with gold cord woven in, as per pattern.

The dress sword belt is to be worn with epaulettes, etc.

The service sword belt for all officers shall be of plain black glazed leather, not less than one inch and a half nor more than two inches wide, with slings of the same not less than one half inch wide nor more than three quarters of an inch wide, and a hook in the forward ring to suspend the sword. Belt plate of yellow gilt in front, two inches in diameter. The belt to be worn over the coat.

Regulations Governing the Uniform of Officers of the United States Navy, 1883 (pp14,15) extensive changes plates I, II and III

Sword-Belt
Full Dress
For the Admiral and Vice Admiral, the belt shall be a dark navy blue cloth with a gold-embroidered stripe one quarter of an inch wide on each edge and one strip of gold embroidered white oak leaves, one half inch wide, running through the center, as per pattern. The sling straps to be of blue cloth with a gold embroidered stripe one eighth of an inch wide on each edge as per pattern (Plate I).

For rear admirals and commodores, the belt shall be a dark navy blue cloth with a gold-embroidered stripe, one quarter of an inch wide on each edge and one of the same width in the center. The sling straps to be of blue cloth with three gold embroidered stripes one eighth of an inch wide, arranged as on the belt.(Plate I).

For captains and commanders, the belt shall be a dark navy blue silk webbing with seven one sixteenth inch gold lace stripes woven as per pattern (Plate II)

For lieutenant commanders and lieutenants, the belt shall be a dark navy blue webbing with five one sixteenth inch gold lace stripes woven as per pattern (Plate II)

For lieutenants (junior grade) and ensigns, the belt shall be a dark navy blue webbing with three one sixteenth inch gold lace stripes woven as per pattern (Plate II)

Sword Slings
Staff officers shall wear the same belt and slings as are prescribed for line officers with whom they have relative rank.

1883 Pattern graphic

Dress Undress and Service Dress

For all officers shall be of plain black leather, not less than one inch and a half nor more than two inches wide, with slings of the same not less than one-half inch wide nor more than three-quarters of an inch wide, and a hook in the forward ring to suspend the sword. Belt-plate of yellow gilt in front, two inches in diameter.

Regulations Governing the Uniform of Commissioned Officers, Warrant Officers, and Enlisted Men of the Navy of the United States,1886 (p14) plates xxviii,xxix,xxx,xxxl - text same as 1883

Regulations Governing the Uniform of Commissioned Officers, Warrant Officers, and Enlisted Men of the Navy of the United States With Plates, 1897 (p 19) same as 1886 - added Special full dress and evening dress plus slight change in undress 1 5/8 nor more than 2 inches wide

**U.S. Navy Department. Regulations Governing the Uniform of Commissioners Officers, Warrant Officers and Enlisted Men of the Navy of the United States, 1905
(p32) plates xvii and xix**

Full Dress Belt.(Pls XVIII and XIX)

For the Admiral of the Navy - to be of dark navy-blue cloth, embroidered on the edges with a gold stripe 1/2 inch wide, in the center with one half that width, Sling straps of

1905 Pattern graphic

dark blue navy cloth embroidered on each edge with a gold stripe 1/4 inch wide and in the center one half that width.

For officers of the rank of rear admiral - the same as above but the stripes on the edge of the belt to be 1/4 inch wide; sling straps to have three 1/8-inch stripes arranged as on the belt

For officers of the rank of captain or commander - to be of *dark navy- blue silk webbing with seven gold stripes one sixteenth inch wide, woven according to pattern; sling straps double, 3/4 inch wide, with buckle*

For officers of the rank of lieutenant commander or lieutenant - to be of *dark navy- blue silk webbing with five gold stripes one sixteenth inch wide, woven according to pattern; sling straps double, 3/4 inch wide, with buckle*

For commissioned officers below the rank of lieutenant, junior grade, except those as hereinafter noted - to be of *dark navy- blue silk webbing with three gold stripes one sixteenth inch wide, woven according to pattern; sling straps double, 3/4 inch wide, with buckle*

Mountings for full dress belt and sling straps to be as shown in Plate XIX p 33

UNDRESS BELT. (PLs XVII and XIX)

For all officers except chaplains: to be of plain black grain leather, not less than 1 5/8 inch nor more than two inches wide, with sling straps of the same not less than 1/2 inch nor more 3/4 inch wide, and attached to the belt as shown for the full dress belt, Plate XVIII; mountings of belt the same as for the full dress belt except the sling straps to have no buckles, The belt plate or buckle to be of yellow gilt in front, two inches in diameter, conforming to pattern.

Uniform Regulations, United States Navy 1913 (Revised to January 15, 1917), as a rev to 1913 - plate 18 same as 1913

U.S. Navy Uniform Regulations,1941

2-72. Full Dress Belt. - This article shall be made of blue-black webbing with gold stripes, backed by black grain leather and fittings. (See Plate 27.)

2-73. Undress Belt. - This article shall consist of plain black leather and fittings. (See Plate 27.)

2-88. Belt, Full Dress: The full dress belt shall be worn by all commissioned officers (except chaplains and chief warrant officers), and shall be of dark navy-blue webbing, backed by black leather, 1 3/4 inches wide, and fastened with a gold plated buckle, 2 inches in diameter, marked as follows:
(1) Officers of Flag Rank. - Three woven gold stripes, each 1/4 inch wide, the two outer stripes in the upper and lower edges, respectively, the third one in the middle; sling straps to be 7/8 inch wide, with three 1/4-inch gold woven stripes, one on each edge and one in the middle.
(2) Officers of the Rank of Captain and Commander.- The same as for officers of flag rank except that there shall be seven gold stripes, each 1/16 inch wide in the belt, and on the sling strap, three 1/16-inch stripes.
(3) Officers of and Below the Rank of Lieutenant Commander. - The same as paragraph (2), but with five gold stripes on the belt and no middle stripe in the sling strap. (See Plate 27.)

2-89. Belt, Undress. - Plain black grain leather, 2 inches wide, with plain sling straps of the same material, 3/4 inch wide, buckle and mounting same as full-dress belt, no special rank markings. (See Plate 27.)

Appendix B:
Excerpts from U.S. Marine Corps
Belt Plate Regulations 1798-1900

Introduction

This appendix contains excerpts from Marine Corps Uniform Regulations and Orders for the period 1798 to 1900.

Excerpts - McClellan, Edwin North, *Uniforms of the American Marines, 1775 to 1932*, Part One, First Edition, September 30, 1932. (original manuscript).

Officers
First printed Uniform Order – October 14, 1805

Side Arms, yellow mounted sabers with Gilt scabbard worn over the Sash. Black belts with yellow mounting.

Belt revised by Order of December 16, 1805
Officers to wear white cross belts with gilt plates

April 19, 1810 Uniform Order
Side Arms – yellow- mounted sabers with Gilt scabbards, & white crossbelts with Gilt plates.

May 11, 1821 Uniform Order
White leather belts across the shoulders

May 15, 1821 Uniform Order
White cross belts, with Gilt plates, and an Eagle in relief

August 25, 1821 printed Uniform Order
scarlet sash, a black leather waist belt, with yellow mountings…

January 30 and May 3 1825
White cross belt with a gilt breast plate, scarlet sash made of silk…

Enlisted Men
October 17, 1798
Not to have the red belts more than two inches wide…

October 26, 1798
Naval buttons to all Viz an Eagle with a shield on the left wing, enclosing a foul anchor. Drummers and Fifers… red cloth coat with blue belt edged with common yellow livery…

January 5, 1801
The red belt must be narrow and made agreeable to the last pattern.

June 9 1805
Contract with Messrs Innes and Kinsey, for twenty-five Sword Belts, of the same leather, width etc., as those they are to furnish for the cartouche boxes. (p37)

March 8, 1806
Some enlisted men were wearing white belts on parade. It appears that while white belts had been adopted in the United States, men from the Enterprize (sic) were not aware of the change. (noted by Captain Anthony Gale to Commodore John Rodgers as if it was a problem). (p43)

October 11, 1813
"buff" belts for enlisted men have been positively for many years directed as part of our accoutrements – there is also reference to buff belts and belt plates in correspondence of the period. (p51)

October 11, 1813
Letter citing Issue about some marines wearing black belts as opposed to buff belts. (p54)

May 29, 1824
Order for white waist belts issued.

January 30 and May 3 1825

White cross belt with a gilt breast plate, scarlet sash made of silk….(p87)

***Dress of the Officers, Non-Commissioned Officers, Musicians and Privates, of the Marine Corps of the United States,* July 1, 1839**

Sword belt – White leather, two inches wide, with sliding frog, to be worn around the waist, over the coat and clasped in front; clasp, according to the a pattern to be furnished by the Quartermasters Department.

23 January 1840 Order - Headquarters of the Marine Corps Adjutant and Inspectors Office

6. Belt. The undress belt to be of black patent leather; the sword to be suspended by black patent leather; swivels of brass to receive the sword.

7. Plate for the belts to be of plain brass of oblong form, three inches in length and two inches wide, with a gold wreath of raised work within it; German text letters "USM" of silver (like raised work) of the same pattern and dimensions as the work on the fatigue cap.

1839 Pattern graphic

Regulations for the Uniforms & Dress of the Navy and Marine Corps of the United States, 1852. (8 March 1852)

Sword-Belt
White leather, two inches wide, with sliding frog, to be worn round the waist, over the coat, and clasped in front: clasp, according to a pattern to be furnished by the Quartermasters Department.

plates include above USMC plate and button

Regulations for the Uniform & Dress of the Marine Corps of the United States, October 1859

Sword Belt
For all Officers. – A waist belt not less than one and one-half inches, nor more than two inches wide, to be worn over the sash; the sword to be suspended from it by slings of the same material as the belt, attached to the belt, upon which the sword may be hung (See Plate Fig. 12)
For the Commandant – Of Russia leather, with three stripes of gold embroidery; the slings embroidered on both sides; or the same belt as to be immediately prescribed for all other officers.

For all other Officers – Of glazed white leather

Sword Belt Plate

For all Officers – Gilt rectangular, two inches wide, with a raised bright rim, a wreath of laurel encircling the Arms of the United States; eagle, shield, edge of cloud, and rays, bright (See Plate Fig. 13)

Belts
All enlisted men shall wear white waist belts of the French pattern, with the French clasp and knapsack sliding slings…

(For Pattern of Belt, complete, see pattern in the Quartermaster's Offcie, Head Quarters)

1864. (Schuyler Hartley & Graham)
Sword Belt
516. *For All officers.* – A waist belt not less than one and one half inches, nor more than two inches wide to be worn over the sash: the sword to be suspended from it by slings as the same material as the belt with a hook attached to the belt, upon which the sword may be hung.

317. *For the Commandant.* – Of Russia leather, with three stripes of gold embroidery: the slings embroidered on both sides, or the same belt as to be immediately prescribed for all other officers...

318. *For All Other Officers.* – Of white glazed leather

Sword Belt Plate

319. *For all Officers.* – Gilt rectangular, two inches wide, with a raised bright rim, a wreath of laurel encircling the Arms of the "United States": eagle, shield, scroll, edge of cloud and rays, bright.

Regulations for the Uniform & Dress of the Marine Corps of the United States, 1875

Sword Belt

For Field and Company Officers: Of crimson and gold lace interwoven, one and a half inches wide; lined with white morocco leather, showing edges of one eighth of an inch white; through the centre of the belt a stripe of crimson silk three-sixteenths of an inch wide: slings of same material and design (See Figure 1 Plate 5). This belt to be worn with full dress only.

Belt- Plate

For all officers: Gilt. rectangular, two and one eighth inches wide by three and one-eighth inches long, with a raised bright rim: a wreath of laurel encircling the "Arms of the United States": eagle, shield, scroll, stars, edge of clouds and rays silvered. (see Plate 5)

Sword Belt and Plate

For all Officers: A white pattern leather belt, not less than one and one half nor more than two inches wide. Style of belt, slings and brass mountings to be the same as the full dress belt. Belt Plate same as described for full-dress belt.

Regulations Governing the Uniforms, Dress, and Equipments, etc., of the United States Marine Corps, 1900

FULL DRESS SWORD BELT

For Brigadier General, Commandant, and all line officers: Of No. 1 Marine Corps gold lace, crimson and gold interwoven, one and one-half inches wide, through the center of which is run a strip of crimson silk three-sixteenths of an inch wide; belt to be lined with white morocco leather, showing edges of one-eighth of an inch wide. Slings of same material and design, best gold lace to be three-fourths of an inch wide, and to show one-sixteenth of an inch of leather on either side.

BELT PLATE

For Brigadier General, Commandant, and all line officers: Gilt, rectangular, two and one-eighth inches wide by three and one-eighth inches long, with a raised bright rim; a wreath of laurel encircling the "Arms of the United States": eagle, shield, scroll, stars, edge of clouds, and rays silvered.

UNDRESS SWORD BELT AND PLATE

Brigadier General, Commandant, and all line officers: A white patent leather belt, two inches wide. Style of belt, belt plate, size of slings, and brass mounting to be the same as prescribed for full-dress belt.

Fig. 13.

1859 Pattern graphic

Endnotes

Chapter 2

1. Albert, Alphaeus H., *Record of American Uniform and Historical Buttons, Bicentennial Edition*, SCS Publications and O'Donnell Publications, Virginia, 1977, pp86-87.
2. Neeser, Robert W., *Statistical and Chronological History of the United States Navy 1775-1907*, Volume II, Burt Franklin, New York, 1970 reprint, p2.
3. *Uniform for the Navy of the United States of America*, Washington, D.C., War Department, 1797.
4. Tuite, Peter, *U.S. Naval Officers, Their Swords and Dirks*, Andrew Mowbray Incorporated, Publishers, Lincoln, RI 2004, p235.
5. *The Uniform Dress of the Captains and Certain Other Officers of the Navy of the United States*, Washington Navy Department, 1802.
6. Tuite, p228
7. Tuite, p24
8. Tuite, p31
9. Tuite, p35
10. O'Donnell, Michael J. and Campbell, J. Duncan, *American Military Belt Plates*, O'Donnell Publications, Alexandria, Virginia 1996.
11. O'Donnell, see plate 982, p523.
12. O'Donnell see plates 981 and 982, pp582-583.
13. Albert NA 22 through 24, pp90-91.
14. Tuite, pp139-148.
15. Callahan, Edward W., *List of Officers of the Navy of the United States and of the Marine Corps from 1775 to 1900*, L.R. Hamersly & Co., New York, 1901, p84.
16. Callahan, p62.
17. Hamilton, John D., *So Nobly Distinguished, Congressional Swords for Sailing Masters and Midshipmen in the War of 1812*, Man at Arms, Volume seven, number 2, March/April 1985, Andrew Mowbray Inc. Publishers, Lincoln, RI. This article contains an image of a Congressional Sword Belt on black leather.
18. Rickard, J., *Sea Fencibles, 1798-1810*, January 25, 2006. http://www.historyofwar.org/articles/weapons_sea_fencibles.html.
19. *Membership Certificate for the Boston Sea Fencibles, 1830*. This certificate admits Winslow W. Seaver of Boston to the Sea Fencibles.
20. Callahan, p437
21. O'Donnell see plate 130, p90
22. O'Donnell pp80-90
24. O'Donnell see plate 138, p94
25 O'Donnell see plate 139, p94
26. Robinson, Admiral Samuel Murray, USN retired, *A Brief History of the Texas Navies*, presented by the Sons of the Republic of Texas, Houston, Texas, 1961.
27. O'Donnell, see plate 611, p410.

Chapter 3

1. *Uniform for the Navy of the United States of America*, Washington, D.C., War Department, 1797.
2. *The Uniform Dress of the Captains and Certain Other Officers of the Navy of the United States*, Washington Navy Department, 1802.
3. *Uniform Regulations for United States Navy, 1820* (May 10, 1820).
4. Tily, James C., *Uniforms of the United States Navy, 1820*, Journal of the Company of Military Collector & Historians, Vol. XXVII, No. 2 Summer 1975, pp70-75.
5. *Rules of the Navy Department, Regulating the Civil Administration of the Navy of the United States*, Printed at the Globe Office by Francis P. Blair, Washington, 1832.
6. Tuite, Peter, *U.S. Naval Officers, Their Swords and Dirks*, Andrew Mowbray Incorporated, Publishers, Lincoln RI 2004, p155.
7. Callahan, Edward W., *List of Officers of the Navy of the United States and of the Marine Corps from 1775 to 1900*, L.R. Hamersly & Co., New York, 1901, p84.

Chapter 4

1. *Regulations for the Uniforms and Dress of the Navy of the United States, 1841*, J.&G.S. Gideon, Printers
2. *Description of the Sword Belts to be in future worn over the Coat by Commissioned Officers of the Royal Navy, and by other Officers ranking with Commissioned Officers*, The Nautical Magazine, published by Brown Son & Ferguson, Glasgow, Vol. 1, August 1832, p335.
3. Jarrett, Dudley, *British Naval Dress*, J.M. Dent and Sons Ltd., Aldine House, Bedford Street, London, 1960, pp83-87.
4. Christies Auction Sale 5924, Lot 129, A Pair of Royal Navy Captains Epaulettes with waist belt marked for: *J. Salter/73 Strand*.
5. Button usage date ranges provided by Bruce Bazelon and Bob French.

Chapter 5

1. Regulations for the Uniforms & Dress of the Navy and Marine Corps of the United States, Philadelphia, Collins, 1852, p7.
2. Tuite, Peter, *U.S. Naval Officers, Their Swords and Dirks*, Andrew Mowbray Incorporated, Publishers, Lincoln RI 2004, p100.
3. Tuite, p101
4. Callahan, Edward W., *List of Officers of the Navy of the United States and of the Marine Corps from 1775 to 1900*, L.R. Hamersly & Co., New York, 1901, p475.
5. Tuite, p100
6. Dudley, William S, *Going South; U.S. Navy Officer Resignations & Dismissals on the Eve of the Civil War*, Naval Historical Foundation, Washington, DC, 1981, pp18-19, table III.
7. *Uniform for the United States Navy*, prepared under the direction of the Secretary of the Navy, Washington, GPO, 1869, p12.
8. *Regulations Governing the Uniform of the United States Navy, 1883*, Washington, GPO, 1883, p14 and plate I.

9. O'Donnell, p599

10. Callahan, p500

11. Tuite, p171

12. Wikipedia website at en.wikipedia.org/wiki/United_States_Navy_officer_rank_insignia.

13. 1869 *Uniform Regulations*, p12.

14. Navy Department, *Uniform for Officers of the United States Navy as prescribed in General Order of The Secretary of the Navy, July 31, 1862 (with appendix)*, Tomes, Son & Melvain, New York, 1863, p5.

15. Navy Department, *Uniform for Officers of the United States navy as prescribed in regulations for the uniform of the U.S Navy, Jan. 28, 1864*, Tomes, Melvain, New York, 1864, p29.

16. Navy Department, *Regulations for the Uniform of the United States Navy*, December 1, 1866, Government Printing Office, p12 and plate 28.

17. O'Donnell, p396

18. *Illustrated Catalogue of Civil War Military Goods*, Schuyler, Hartley & Graham, 1864, Reproduction by Dover Publications, Inc., New York, 1985, No. 329, navy belt plate, p103.

19. Callahan, p392

20. Tuite, p167

21. Bazelon, Bruce S., *Horstmanns: the Enterprise of Military Equipage*, REF Typesetting & Publishing, Inc., 9400 Fairview Avenue, Manassas, VA, 20110, 1997, p157.

22. Callahan, p527

23. Reilly, John, *Proud Beginnings: History of Warrant Officers in the US Navy*, Naval Historical Center website, Traditions of the Naval Service.

24. Wikipedia website at en.wikipedia.org/wiki/United_States_Navy_officer_rank_insignia.

25. *1869 Navy Uniform Regulations*, p12.

26. Jacobsen, Jacques Noel Jr., *Horstmann Bros. and Co., Catalogue of Military Goods for 1877*, Pioneer Press, Union City TN, 38261, Second printing, 1989, U.S. Navy Belt Plate-1313, full size.

27. *Regulations for the Government of the Navy of the United States, 1876*, Washington, GPO, 1877, p13

28. U.S. Navy Department. *Regulations Governing the Uniform of Commissioned Officers, Warrant Officers and Enlisted Men of the Navy of the United States, 1905*, Wash, DC: GPO, 1905, p32, plates xvii and xix.

29. *1869 Navy Uniform Regulations*, p12

30. Callahan, p564

31. Tuite, p195

32. Bazelon, p67

33. *Regulations Governing the Uniform of Commissioned Officers, Warrant Officers, and Enlisted Men of the Navy of the United States*, Washington, GPO, 1886, p14.

34. *Regulations Governing the Uniform of Commissioned Officers, Warrant Officers, and Enlisted Men of the Navy of the United States With Plates*, Washington, GPO, 1897, p19.

35. *1905 Uniform Regulations*, plate XIX.

36. *Uniform Regulations, United States Navy 1913* (Revised to January 15, 1917), Wash, DC: GPO, 1917, p43, plates 1, 2, and 3.

37. 1913 Navy Uniform Regulations, p43.

38. 1869 Navy Uniform Regulations, p12.

39. Tuite, p191

40. Callahan, p434

41. Callahan, p53

42. Tuite, p198

43. Bazelon, p74

44. *U.S. Navy Uniform Regulations, 1941*, Navy Department, Bureau of Navigation, plate 27.

Chapter 6

1. Listings of USMC officers by rank, name, and station as contained in the U.S. Navy Registers for 1840, 1849, 1852, and 1854.

2. Cureton, Lt. Col, Charles H. and Sullivan, David M., *The Civil War Uniforms of the United States Marine Corps: The Regulations of 1859*, R. James Bender Publishing, San Jose California, 2009, p13.

3. Cureton, Lt. Col. Charles, H., USMCR (Ret.), *Early Marine Corps Swords*, The Bulletin of the American Society of Arms Collectors, Number 93, 2006, c1799 portrait of First Lieutenant Jonathan Church, Figure 29, p120; c1809 portrait of First Lieutenant Lee Massey, Figure 31, p121.

4. McClellan, Edwin North, *Uniforms of the American Marines, 1775 to 1932, Part One*, First Edition, September 30, 1932 (original manuscript), p39.

5. McClellan, p70.

6. Cureton, Lt Colonel Charles, image of Lt Donald Sutherland c1839-1850 wearing white belt with navy belt plate, p67; image of Lt Phillip Clayton Kennedy c1861 wearing navy belt plate with black belt, p165; image of Major and Paymaster William Worthington Russell c1855 wearing black belt with navy belt plate, p143.

7. *The Eagle, Globe, and Anchor 1868-1968*, History and Museums Division, Headquarters U.S. Marine Corps, Washington, D.C., pp 14,15 (later versions show author; Colonel John A. Driscoll USMCR).

8. McClellan cites red belts on p 8, but more recent research by Lt. Colonel Charles Cureton indicates that these belts were black.

9. McClellan, p20

10. McClellan, p37

11. McClellan, p43

12. McClellan, p51

13. McClellan, p70

14. Bazelon, Bruce S., & McGuinn, William F., *A Directory of American Military Goods Dealers & Makers 1785-1915*, REF Typesetting & Publishing, Inc., Manassas, Virginia, p3.

15. Bazelon, p76, Edmund Kinsey had a USMC contract as early as 11 February 1808 for 100 caps.

16. Bazelon, p49

17. Bazelon, p35, Robert Dingee and his brother Robert were the most prominent New York suppliers of military insignia and accoutrements during the first half of the nineteenth century. Among other things he contributed to the adoption of the 1828 bayonet belt, scabbard, and belt plate.

18. McClellan, p77

19. McClellan, p78

20. McClellan, p84

21. McClellan, p87

22. McClellan, p88

23. Campbell, J. Duncan and Howell, Edgar M., *American Military Insignia*, Smithsonian Institution, Washington D.C., 1963 Smithsonian Bulletin, p22.

24. O'Donnell, Michael J. & Campbell, J. Duncan, *American Military Belt Plates*, O'Donnell Publications, Alexandria, Virginia, May 1996, p69.

24. O'Donnel, p97

25, O'Donnel, p584

26. Cureton, Lt. Colonel Charles, p278

27. Dorsey, R. Stephen, *American Military and Naval Belts, 1812-1902*, Collectors Library, Eugene Oregon, 2002, p194.

28. Cureton, Lt. Colonel Charles, p279.

29. Cureton, Lt. Colonel Charles, p279, and Campbell, figure 65, p37. Although not defined as a Marine shoulder plate in Campbell, it's the identical plate shown in Cureton.

30. Campbell, p23

31. O'Donnel, p67

32. O'Donnel, p585

33. *Regulations for the Uniforms & Dress of the Navy and Marine Corps of the United States*. Phila: Collins, 1852, Plate entitled *Marine Corps*.

34. Cureton, Lt. Colonel Charles, officers and enlisted men were wearing the eagle on slanted anchor hat plate without embellishment as shown by the image of 2nd Lt John Cash c1850, p68, and the image of a Corporal in his 1839 dress with dress cap in the mid-1850s, p62.

35. Cureton, Lt. Colonel Charles, p242.

36. *Regulations for the Uniform & Dress of the Marine Corps of the United States, October 1859*, First edition, Charles Desilver, Publisher and Bookseller, No. 714 Chestnut Street, Philadelphia, p8 under *Belts*.

37. O'Donnell, plate 985, p586.

38. O'Donnell, plate 135, p92.

39. *Dress of the Officers, Non-Commissioned Officers, Musicians and Privates, of the Marine Corps of the United States*, Adjutant and Inspectors Office, Washington, July 1, 1839, p5 under *Sword* and *Sword Belt*.

40. *1852 U.S. Navy Uniform Regulations*, p7.

41. Gavin, William G., *Accoutrement Plates North and South 1861-1865*, second edition, George Shumway Publisher, York, Pennsylvania, 1975, pp234-235.

42. O'Donnell, p587

43. 1859 Marine Corps Uniform Regulations, pp5-6 under *Sword Belt*.

44. Campbell, p48 and 49

45. *Illustrated Catalogue of Civil War Military Goods, Schuyler, Hartley & Graham, 1864*, Reproduction by Dover Publications, Inc., New York, 1985, p47.

46. *Uniform Regulations United States Marine Corps, Together with the Uniform Regulations Common to Both The U.S. Navy And Marine Corps*, Headquarters, United States Marine Corps, 1912, Washington, Government Printing Office, 1913, plate 19.

Chapter 7

1. *Official Records of the Union and Confederate Navies in the War of the Rebellion*, Series II, Volume 2, Navy Department, Washington, 1921, p44.

2. Dudley, William, *Going South: U.S. Navy Officer Resignations & Dismissals on the Eve of the Civil War*, Naval Historical Foundation, Washington, D.C., 1981, p18 and 19, Table III. Note that additional USN officers and rates joined the Confederate Navy later in the war.

3. *Official Records of the Union and Confederate Navies in the War of the Rebellion*, p57.

4. Scharf, J. Thomas, *History of the Confederate States Navy*, Fairfax Press, 1977, p41 shows 3,674 enlisted men in 1864, while other sources show as many as 4500 enlisted men. A table on p14 shows 460 officers and rates from the South and 713 from the North, while other sources show lower numbers.

5. *Uniform and Dress of the Army of the Confederate States*, Chas. H. Wynne, Printer, Richmond, 1861.

6. *North South Traders Civil War* - Steve Sylvia article.

7. O'Donnell, Michael J. & Campbell, J. Duncan, *American Military Belt Plates*, O'Donnell Publications, Alexandria, Virginia, May 1996, pp 171-177.

8. Gavin, William G., *Accoutrement Plates North and South 1861-1865*, second edition, George Shumway Publisher, York, Pennsylvania, 1975, p128, cites: *the plate is with the original belt and sword, the latter having been supplied by Firmin...*

9. *Register of Officers of the Confederate States Navy, 1861-1865*, J.M. Carroll & Company, Mattituck New York, 1983, p139, as supplemented by web searches.

10. *Register of Officers of the Confederate States Navy, 1861-1865*, p39, as supplemented by web searches.

11. *Register of Officers of the Confederate States Navy, 1861-1865*, p151, as supplemented by web searches.

12. Riling, R. and Halter, R., *Uniform and Dress, Army and Navy of the Confederate States of America*, Confederate States of America War Department and Confederate States of America Navy Department, reproduction, New Hope, PA, 1952.

Bibliography

Albert, Alphaeus H., *Record of American Uniform and Historical Buttons, Bicentennial Edition,* SCS Publications and O'Donnell Publications, Virginia, 1977

Bazelon, Bruce S, & McGuinn, William F., *A Directory of American Military Goods Dealers & Makers 1785-1915,* REF Typesetting & Publishing, Inc., Manassas, Virginia

Callahan, Edward W., *List of Officers of the Navy of the United States and of the Marine Corps from 1775 to 1900,* L.R. Hamersly & Co., New York, 1901

Campbell, J. Duncan and Howell, Edgar M., *American Military Insignia,* Smithsonian Institution, Washington D.C., 1963

Comfort, Sim, *Naval Swords & Dirks, Volume I,* Sim Comfort Associates, 2008

Cureton, Lt. Col. Charles H. and Sullivan, David M., *The Civil War Uniforms of the United States Marine Corps: The Regulations of 1859,* R. James Bender Publishing, San Jose California. 2009

Cureton, Lt. Col. Charles, H., USMCR (Ret.), *Early Marine Corps Swords, The Bulletin of the American Society of Arms Collectors,* Number 93, 2006

Dorsey, R. Stephen, *American Military and Naval Belts, 1812-1902,* Collectors Library, Eugene Oregon, 2002

Driscoll, Colonel John A. USMCR, *The Eagle, Globe, and Anchor 1868-1968,* History and Museums Division, Headquarters U.S. Marine Corps, Washington, D.C.

Dudley, William, *Going South: U.S. Navy Officer Resignations & Dismissals on the Eve of the Civil War,* Naval Historical Foundation, Washington, D.C., 1981

Gavin, William G., *Accoutrement Plates North and South 1861-1865,* second edition, George Shumway Publisher, York Pennsylvania, 1975

Hamilton, John D., *So Nobly Distinguished, Congressional Swords for Sailing Masters and Midshipmen in the War of 1812,* Man at Arms, Volume seven, number 2, March/April, 1985

Illustrated Catalogue of Civil War Military Goods, Schuyler, Hartley & Graham, 1864, Reproduction by Dover Publications, Inc., New York, 1985

Jacobsen, Jacques Noel Jr., *Horstmann Bros. and Co., Catalogue of Military Goods for 1877,* Pioneer Press, Union City TN, 38261, Second printing, 1989,

Jarrett, Dudley, *British Naval Dress,* J.M. Dent and Sons Ltd., Aldine House, Bedford Street, London, 1960

McClellan, Edwin North, *Uniforms of the American Marines, 1775 to 1932,* Part One, First Edition, September 30, 1932 (original manuscript)

Neeser, *Statistical and Chronological History of the United States Navy 1775-1907,* Volume II, Burt Franklin, New York, 1970 reprint

O'Donnell, Michael J. & Campbell, J. Duncan, *American Military Belt Plates,* O'Donnell Publications, Alexandria, Virginia, May 1996

Powell, John T. *Naval Officers Belt Plate, c 1800-1815,* Journal of the Company of Military Collector & Historian, Vol. XXVII, No. 3 Fall 1975

Reilly, John, *Proud Beginnings: History of Warrant Officers in the US Navy,* Naval Historical Center website, Traditions of the Naval Service

Tily, Captain James C., (CEC USN), Military Dress, *A Reproduction of the 1830 Naval Uniform Regulations,* Journal of the Company of Military Collector & Historian, Vol. XI, No. 2 Summer 1959

Tily, James C, *Uniforms of the United States Navy, 1820,* Journal of the Company of Military Collector & Historian, Vol. XXVII, No. 2 Summer 1975

Tuite, Peter, *U.S. Naval Officers, Their Swords and Dirks,* Andrew Mowbray Incorporated, Publishers, Lincoln, RI 2004

Uniform and Dress of the Army of Confederate States, Richmond: Chas. H. Wynne, Printer, 94 Main Street, 1861

U.S. Navy Uniform Regulations

Uniform for the Navy of the United States of America, Washington, D.C., War Department, 1797

The Uniform Dress of the Captains and Certain Other Officers of the Navy of the United States, Washington Navy Department, 1802

The Uniform Dress of the Officers of the Navy of the United States, November 15, 1815 (effective January 1, 1814)

Uniform Regulations for United States Navy, 1820 (May 10, 1820)

Rules of the Navy Department, Regulating the Civil Administration of the Navy of the United States, Printed at the Globe Office by Francis P. Blair, Washington 1832

Regulations for the Uniforms and Dress of the Navy of the United States, 1841, J.&G.S. Gideon, Printers

Regulations for the Uniforms & Dress of the Navy and Marine Corps of the United States, Phila: Collins,1852

Navy Department, Uniform for Officers of the United States Navy as prescribed in General Order of The Secretary of the Navy, July 31, 1862 (with appendix), Tomes, Son & Melvain, New York, 1863

Navy Department, Uniform for Officers of the United States Navy as Prescribed in Regulations for the Uniform of the U.S Navy, Jan. 28, 1864, Tomes, Melvain, New York, 1864

Navy Department, Regulations for the Uniform of the United States Navy, December 1, 1866, Government Printing Office

Uniform for the United States Navy, prepared under the direction of the Secretary of the Navy, Washington, Government Printing Office, 1869

Navy Department, Regulations for the Government of the Navy of the United States 1876, Appendix 5, Government Printing Office, 1877

Regulations Governing the Uniform of Officers of the United States Navy, 1883, Washington, GPO, 1883

Regulations Governing the Uniform of Commissioned Officers, Warrant Officers, and Enlisted Men of the Navy of the United States, Washington, GPO, 1886

Regulations Governing the Uniform of Commissioned Officers, Warrant Officers, and Enlisted Men of the Navy of the United States With Plates, Washington, GPO, 1897

U.S. Navy Department. Regulations Governing the Uniform of Commissioners Officers, Warrant Officers and Enlisted Men of the Navy of the United States, 1905. Wash, DC: GPO, 1905

Uniform Regulations, United States Navy 1915 (Revised to January 15, 1917), Wash, DC: GPO, 1917

U.S. Navy Uniform Regulations, 1941, Navy Department, Bureau of Navigation

U.S. Marine Corps Uniform Regulations

Dress of the Officers, Non-Commissioned Officers, Musicians and Privates, of the Marine Corps of the United States, Adjutant and Inspectors Office, Washington, July 1, 1839

Regulations for the Uniform & Dress of the Marine Corps of the United States, October 1859, First edition, Charles Desilver , Publisher and Bookseller, No. 714 Chestnut Street, Philadelphia

Regulations for the Uniform & Dress of the Marine Corps of the United States, 1875, U.S Government Printing Office, Washington, D.C.

Regulations Governing the Uniforms, Dress, and Equipments, etc., of the United States Marine Corps, 1900, U.S Government Printing Office, Washington, D.C.

Uniform Regulations United States Marine Corps, Together with the Uniform Regulations Common to Both The U.S. Navy And Marine Corps, Headquarters, United States Marine Corps, 1912, Washington, Government Printing Office, 1913

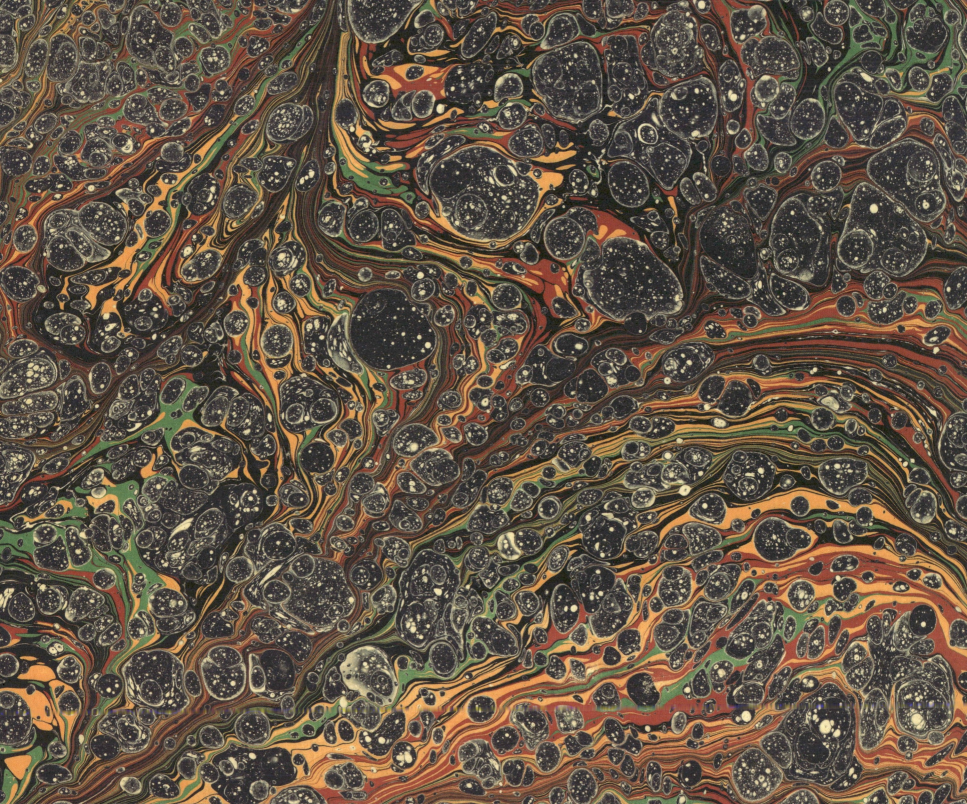